Christians in Oman

Christians in Oman

written as a Durham (U.K.) University Masters Thesis, under the title:

IBĀḌISM IN OMAN

AND DEVELOPMENTS IN THE FIELD

OF CHRISTIAN - MUSLIM RELATIONSHIPS.

June 1992
First Printed November 1995

Second print May 2006

Raymond Frederick Skinner

TOWER PRESS
St Lawrence, London Road
MORDEN, Surrey
SM4 5QT

ISBN No: 0 9527004 0 9

Christians in Oman

Ibāḍism in Oman, and developments in the field of Christian - Muslim relationships

Raymond F. Skinner 1992.
This edition 1995.

ABSTRACT

The purpose of this study is to explore the relationship between Christians and the Ibāḍī of Oman, as a contribution to Christian-Muslim dialogue. The main focus is an assessment of the contribution offered in the past by the small missionary presence, and of the potential scope and areas of dialogue between the recent guest-worker Christian community, and their hosts - a Muslim country growing in international status. The thesis tells the story of a dynamic engagement in dialogue. The history, customs and beliefs of the country will be outlined, with particular emphasis on meeting points with Christian missionaries. The History of the Imāms and Seyyids of Oman by Salīl bin Razik, translated by G.P.Badger and published in 1871, is the source of several more recent works consulted. The Journal of the Arabian Mission of the Reformed Church of America, Neglected Arabia/ Arabia Calling: 1892-1962 and the quarterly The Muslim World (from 1911) have been among other main sources. Some of the many books and articles by Samuel Zwemer have been read; he visited Muscat in Oman on several occasions - his brother Peter contracting a fatal illness while serving there.

The Ibāḍī believe their understanding of Islām to be close to that of the Prophet Muḥammad; individual in faith, they fiercely claim to be orthodox in their interpretation of the Qur'ān, and they are quick to speak out when they think its essential tenets are being compromised. They can therefore perhaps afford to be relaxed when it comes to living alongside those who are not themselves Ibāḍī, and are willing to listen to them with an open mind. Their courteous meeting with the Christians they welcome to their country, offers clues in the wider field of Christian-Muslim relations.

The final section of the book considers some of the key issues in dialogue between Muslim and Christian, and attempts some original thinking in this area, in particular in relation to Christ and time.

Frontspiece: The Lord's Prayer in arabic.

Contents:

Acknowledgements, & Notes on transliteration of Arabic Words	5
Abbreviations	6
Introduction	7
Map of the Sultanate of Oman	10
Chapter 1: Geographical perspectives	11
Chapter 2: An early History of Ibāḍism	16
Chapter 3: Ibāḍism in North Africa and South Arabia	25
Chapter 4: Yaᶜaribi and Al Bu Saᶜīdi to 1900AD/ 1317AH	33
Chapter 5: Christianity in South and East Arabia to 1900AD/ 1317AH	44
Chapter 6: Sultān and Imām 1900-1930AD/ 1317-1349AH	56
Chapter 7: Christians in Oman 1900-1930AD/ 1317-1349AH	61
Chapter 8: Sultān, Imām, and Christian in Oman, since 1930AD/ 1349AH	65
Chapter 9: Dialogue: Folk Religion in Oman	76
Chapter 10: Distinctive doctrines of Ibāḍism	82
Chapter 11: Dialogue with tenets of Ibāḍism	89
Chapter 12: The House of Islām and of War: The Unity of God	101
Appendix: 1: The Gospel of Barnabas	112
2: The Church of the Good Shepherd	121
Bibliography	122

ACKNOWLEDGEMENTS

I am very grateful for the considerable help and encouragement that Professor Edward Hulmes has been, in enabling me to undertake this work: in patient and enthusiastic tutoring, pointing me into various stimulating fields of study and questioning. I am grateful also, for the support of colleagues and friends in the Sultanate of Oman -Government, Church and local community there, and past and present missionaries of the Reformed Church in America; also more recently the parish of Morden, South London.

Thankyou to Bishop Kenneth Cragg, who has been for half a life-time, a source of great inspiration and Christian hope. Thankyou to my parents, who gave me the first name of Ramon Lull; I trust his searching out the pathway of love, will inspire any who read this, to climb higher themselves into the mountain of the Beloved. Thankyou to Dr Aḥmad ᶜUbaydlī for his encouragement, whose own Doctoral thesis on early Ibāḍī history is dedicated to: the 'Lover who has to cross the road of love full of difficulties and slips, who sees hope shining in front of him like a flame while his heart keeps beating like a bell.' (from Ḥusayn al-Miḥdar, a contemporary Yemeni folk poet). Most of all, I thank my wife Hilary, for her unfailing patience, making space for me in crowded days, and for her material encouragement.

Finally to Traidcraft plc, without whose gift of an Amstrad (when I left them as non-executive Chairman), I would not have been able to execute this work.

Notes on the transliteration of Arabic words:

The system of transliteration follows that found in the Encyclopaedia of Islām with the following differences:

th becomes th
dj becomes j
k becomes q.

Dates:

For dates after the Hijrah, the flight from Makkah to Medinah by Muḥammad and his followers, wherever possible the date is first given Anno Domini (AD), then After the Hijrah (AH), so that readers from Christian and Muslim traditions can place events in the most natural time-frame for each. When a date of publication is referred to, the date is given according to A.D. dating only.

ABBREVIATIONS

Qur'ān	ᶜAlī, A. Yusuf, 1975, Text Translation and Commentary of the Holy Qur'ān, Islamic Foundation, Leicester.
EI[1]	Encyclopaedia of Islām, 1913-34, 1st edition, E. J. Brill, Leiden, four volumes.
EI[2]	Encyclopaedia of Islām, 1960-91, 2nd edition, E. J. Brill, Leiden, six volumes to date.
G.B.V.	RAGG, Canon Lonsdale and Laura, 1907, The Gospel of Barnabas, edited and translated from the Italian MS. in the Imperial Library at Vienna, Clarendon Press, Oxford
NA/AC	Neglected Arabia/Arabia Calling: 1892-1962, Journal of the Arabian Mission of the Reformed Church in America. Archive Editions, London
M.W.	The Moslem World, (Muslim World after 1947): ÊA Quarterly Review of Current Events, Literature and thought among Mohammedans and the the Progress of Christian Missions in Moslem Lands, 1911-1938 Editor Samuel M. Zwemer, to 1947 Co-editor with E. E. Calverley. Vols I-VI published by Christian Literature Society for India, London. Vols VII-XXVII by Missionary Review Pub. C., New York. Vols. XXVIII onwards, by Hartford Seminary Found., Hartford, USA.

INTRODUCTION:

The fieldwork for this thesis was undertaken during nearly three years as Anglican Chaplain in Oman; a post which involved travel throughout the Sultanate, with the opportunity of many conversations with Omanis, both of Ibāḍī as well as other Islamic backgrounds. Correspondence and meetings with retired missionaries contribute valuable insights.

Until recently, free discourse and travel has been difficult in Arabia, and remains so in many regions within the peninsular. However in the Sultanate of Oman, there has traditionally been a welcome for the courteous visitor. The expatriate community is allowed to build churches, and its clergy have no restrictions put on them, within the bounds of non-proselytisation. Consequently, unlike most expatriates who usually can explore the great and varied beauty of Oman only on holiday, I was able to travel extensively. The Sultan of Oman's Air Force (S.O.A.F.) and Petrol Development Oman (P.D.O.) enabled me to journey frequently by air, as did Oman Aviation. The coastline, the deserts and mountains of Oman with the contrasting green of its palm-groves each usually with a protecting fort, can be seen from the air in stark contrast to the desert; more important, air travel affords the leisure for conversation. As well as occasionally hitch-hiking, I drove about a hundred thousand kilometres, usually on excellent roads where a 500 k. round trip for an evening meeting or service was not uncommon. Off-road driving in Oman provides as challenging driving conditions as anywhere; again, the opportunity to talk on the journey, as well as at one's destination. Travel by fishing-boat provided a further variation for travel, and meeting.

Oman has welcomed expatriate labour in the careful development of the infra-structure for a modern state. In most towns, small groups of Christians meet in their homes. In most camps, hospitals and clinics, sometimes hidden high up in the mountains, Christian expatriates offered a warm welcome. Omanis also proved unfailingly hospitable, and in so many instances, it became apparent that such friendliness was due to the century of medical care and the school of the Reformed Church in America missionaries.

Much of my time was spent in the Capital Area, involved in varying degrees in the life of many congregations, covering Orthodox and Roman Catholic as well as many Protestant denominations, all drawn from the expatriate community. However, there were frequent meeting points with Omanis socially, and bureaucratically. More occasionally, there were formal opportunities for meeting religious leaders from the host community.

Most contemporary studies of Oman focus on religious issues only in order to draw political conclusions. However:

> 'To a modern Westerner a knowledge of the nuances of classical Islāmic theology might not seem the most vital prerequisite if one is to understand the modernisation of a Middle-Eastern country. Yet the traditional Islamic system embodied the ideology, the value structure, and the aspirations that for centuries prompted men to think and act in certain ways. If one is to have any comprehension of the movement of modernisation in the Middle East - a movement which above all else involves changes or new directions in ideology, values and aspirations - then a knowledge of the traditional Islāmic religious system is most necessary.' [1]

My thesis is, that the dialogue between Muslim and Christian in Oman during the last one hundred years, has been of significance for both future dialogue within Oman, and further afield.

The background to a twentieth century dialogue of Ibāḍī with Christian, begins naturally with a brief geographical description of the country that has originated and nurtured the Ibāḍī tenets of Islam. This is provided in chapter One.

Chapter Two considers the history of the Ibāḍī during the first century of Islām, and the relation between the Ibāḍī with the Khawārij, their links with Basrah and expulsion/ expansion thence. Chapter Three considers the spread of Ibāḍī thought in North Africa and South Arabia. Chapter Four traces the tensions between temporal and spiritual leadership, during the period of the Yaᶜariba Imām beginning 1624 AD/ 1034 AH, followed by the dynasty of the Al Bu Saᶜīd Sultāns who succeeded them, up to 1900 AD/ 1317 AH.

Chapter Five recounts briefly, against the background of the relationship between Sultān and Imām, the history of Christianity in Arabia, more particularly in Oman up to 1900 AD/ 1317 AH. The original objectives of the American Mission (their Muscat station was established in 1892 AD/ 1310 AH) are outlined, and how those began to be worked out through education and medicine. Chapter Six develops the theme of continuing tension between Sultāns and Imām; Chapter Seven, with the presence of Christian missionaries in the background; Chapter Eight traces the interaction between the missionaries and a modernising arab state, together with - since 1970 AD/ 1389 AH - its Christian guest-workers.

Chapter Nine introduces a consideration of religious beliefs in Oman, beginning with aspects of folk religion. Chapter Ten records some key beliefs that distinguish the Ibāḍī from his/her fellow Muslim, particularly those that offer bridges of dialogue between Islām and Christianity. The tentative parallel is drawn, between the Ibāḍī in relation to Islām, and the Protestant or Reformed Christian in relation to Christianity; Ibāḍiyyah retain a 'high' view of the Qur'ān, but think for themselves, and are happy to talk with others "surrendered to God" (Sheikh Aḥmed Zaki Yamāni so allows that description of Professor W. Montgomery Watt).[2] As, I hope, an ecumenically minded Protestant, I cannot explain otherwise the friendliness with which I was received.

Chapter Eleven suggests some areas of dialogue which could be fruitfully followed up - not only in Oman, but in other places where Muslims and Christians are dynamically interacting in their daᶜwah or mission; how Arabs might co-exist as Muslim and Christian; how they should accept each other, as surrendered to God. The final Chapter considers one of the key issues in dialogue between Muslim and Christian, namely the Unity of God in the light of the Christian claim that 'God was in Christ, reconciling the world to Himself.'

An appendix is added concerning the Gospel of Barnabas, which is receiving renewed interest in the Gulf area.

Notes and References:

1. LANDEN, Robert Geran, 1967, Oman since 1856 (Disruptive modernisation in a traditional Arab society). Princeton University Press, USA. pp. xv, 488
2. WATT, W. Montgomery, 1983, Islām and Christianity today. Routledge and Kegan Paul, London, p. ix

The Sultanate of Oman

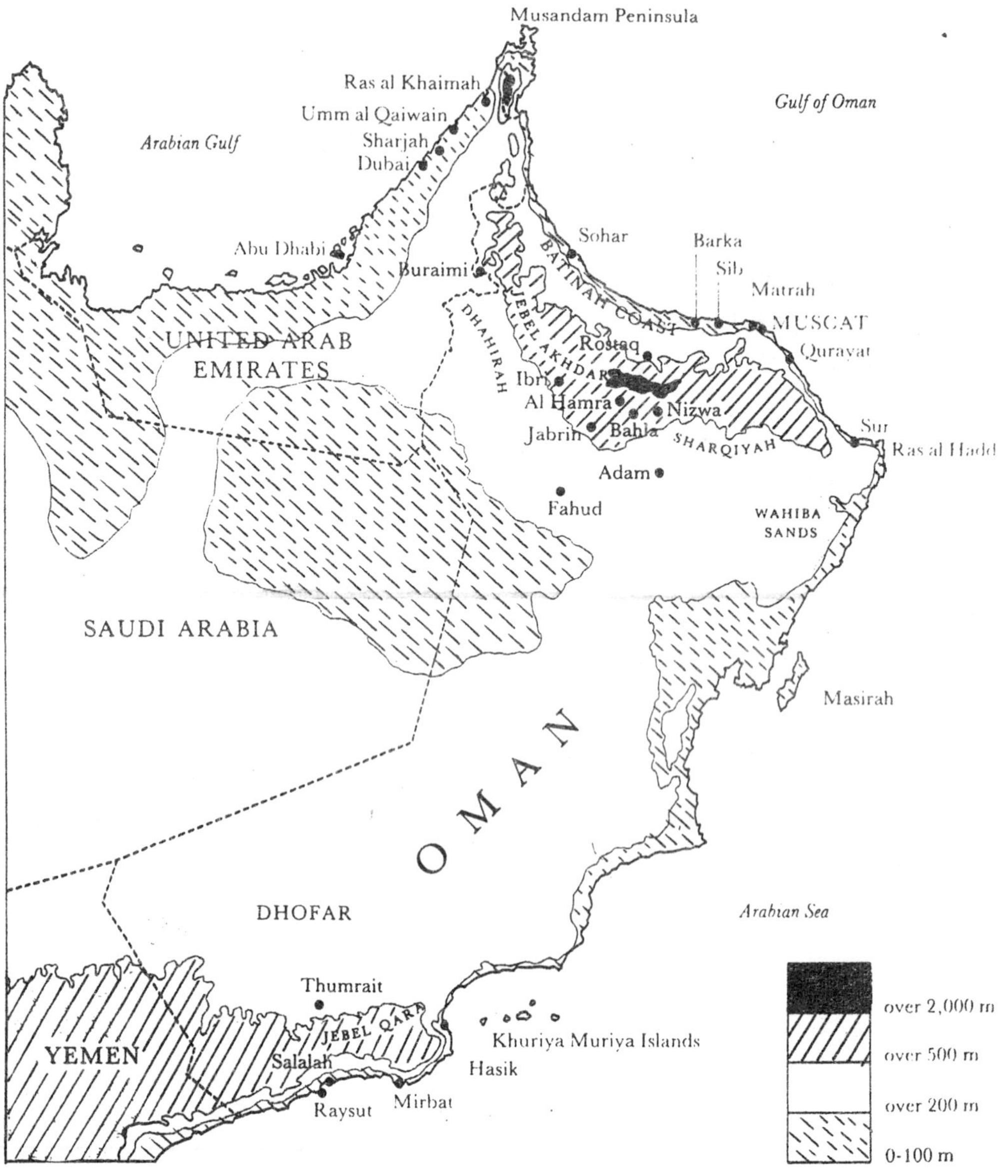

Reproduced from Sea-shells of Oman, with kind permission of Dr Donald and Mrs Eloise Bosch - see note 6 on page 15.

1: Geographical perspectives.

The topography of Oman is perhaps one reason why its people are independent in their religion. Northern Oman, on the eastern side of the Arabian peninsula, is like an island. On one side the sea, on the other Arabia's Empty Quarter. The whole mountain range is called the Hajar, at its heart the Jabal Akhḍar range rising to Jabal al- Shams, the mountain of the sun, 2,980 metres high. The Musandam Peninsula, which itself means the 'anvil', along the Strait of Hormuz, forms the northern tip of the country, separated in the last thirty years from the main land-mass of Oman by 100 kilometres of United Arab Emirates territory.

To the south of the central desert plateau, the narrow coastal plain of Dhofar has a tropical atmosphere, touched by the corner of a monsoon in August and September; this turns the escarpment between sea and desert into a scene reminiscent of the South Downs of England. Coconut palms replace the date palms of the rest of the Sultanate; behind the plain, the mountains rise towards the Yemen border, among them the Jabal al-Qamar, the mountain of the moon. Ra's al Ḥadd forms the eastern promontory of Arabia. The barren island of Masīrah, 60k. long is not far south; its south-eastern pyramid-shaped promontary Ra's Kaydah gives the sense of being at the very edge of the world.

> The Arabs liken the mountains (of northern Oman) to a backbone, calling the area which lies on the Gulf of Oman the bāṭinah or stomach, and the area to the west of the hills the ḍahirah or back. The Bāṭinah consists of a coastal plain built up over the centuries by the outwash from the many wādī which descend from the mountains. This is the principal agricultural and date-growing area, and the palm gardens, watered by wells drawing on subterranean run-off from the hills, stretch northwards from Muscat for some 400 kilometres with scarcely a gap.... The Hajar range is divided by a number of great wādī passes.... Wādī Samail is the greatest and most striking and is regarded as the major divide.... [1]

Muscat is the Capital of Oman. Until Sultan Qaboos took over as ruler from his father in 1971, the physical separation between Muscat and Oman had been very significant. The port of Muscat itself was virtually impregnable, the harbour surrounded by mountains, and low but deeply incised mountains round the little city. To the north, the Bāṭinah coast could be controlled from Muscat, although Ṣuḥār 200k. away, exposed by flat land all round, was sufficiently far to develop its own trading significance, while never having much strategic importance. Along the Bāṭinah coast between, there are many towns and villages. South of Muscat between the mountains, there are smaller coastal settlements, with the occasional plain behind, such as around Quriyat, once famous for its horses. At the southern end of the Hajar lies the fishing and boat-building port of Ṣūr, near Ra's al Ḥadd. Then the flat desert, sand-sea and gravel plain, stretching away south to Ṣalalah, the main town of Dhofar, 1000k south from Muscat.

The population of Oman is 1.6 million; this compares with the other nations of the Arabian peninsular: Saudi Arabia 15 million, Yemen 9.8 million, United Arab Emirates 1.6 million, Bahrein 0.5 million, Qatar 0.5 million, Kuwait 2.1 million.[2] 60% of Kuwait's population was, prior to the invasion by Iraq in August 1990 AD/ Muharram 1411 AH, ex-patriate workers; a smaller proportion of the other states would also have been ex-patriate, Yemen having the smallest number, Oman around 150,000.

The mountains have clearly been a factor in the tribal divisions of Oman. While delineating the territory of Arabian tribes is often difficult, the mountains of Oman form natural barriers. The tribe, or Banī Riyam have long occupied the main Jabal Akhḍar plateau, and its approaches from the south through Tanuf and Birkat al Moz, to the north of Nizwah. To the north below sheer precipices, are the Banī Kharūs in their own spectacular 40k. long wādī named after them; so also, with many other tribes and wadi. Across the more open Wādī Samail south of Barkah, the Banī Ruwāha live, whose senior Sheikhs are the Khalīlī family, from whom came Imām Muḥammad bin ᶜAbdullāh al-Khalīlī (1920-1953 AD/ 1338-1373 AH), as well as the present Grand Mufti of Oman. However, it must be noted that:

> Once a tribe has received its identity and is recognised by the others, a quite informal and accidental matter, it will usually grow and perhaps give rise to daughter tribes.... most of the older existing descent-group tribes contain sections which are of entirely different origin to the rest of the tribe. Eventually a situation like that of the Banī Riyam may develop where the bulk of the tribe is in fact non-Riyami.[3]

Tribal solidarity, ᶜ<u>aṣabīyah</u>, arises out of the basic human need for protection against attack on persons and property. Certainly in Oman, ᶜ<u>aṣabīyah</u> extends more widely than the family, and through several generations:

> The living relatives of your clan continuously change in time, but their relationship is maintained by reference to the supposed eponymous founder of the clan, the man designated as a <u>jadd</u>, which means both the clan founder, and your grandfather...[4]

The main occupation of Omanis has been agriculture. Under the date-palms of the Bāṭinah, interspersed with a few lime-trees banana and mango-trees, alfalfa for goat feed is grown, together with some cereals. With careful terracing and irrigation, the sides of <u>wādī</u> have been made to support similar crops. Sometimes, high up in the Jabal Akhḍar, sudden flashes of brilliant fruit-blossom catch the eye, and tiny vineyards produce a small sour grape. Many more terraces have been painstakingly cut out of the rock than are cultivated today.

Local tradition is that King Solomon had a hand in designing the intricate channels, or fulūj that have been so much a feature of Oman's life; they were certainly developed extensively by the Persians over two thousand years ago. Sometimes running deep underground for 30k. or more, or around the sides of rocky outcrops, and across intricately-built viaducts, the fulūj require constant maintenance. As they flow through a village, stages for different usage are carefully arranged: drinking water, personal hygiene, clothes' washing, and finally crop irrigation, as are the times each family is allowed the flow of water to reach its own palm-grove. Control is effectively operated with gaps in the falj wall, blocked and unblocked with large stones and rags. In a thousand and more long hot summers, The majlis or meeting room of any Omani fort or principal home or beit in a village, has probably had the water rights, timing, and speed of flow, to each and every palm-garden of a community, and any variations to the rule, as the main topic of debate. Could such essential conversation be compared with that of the British, in their pre-occupation with the weather?

> Each community dependent on a single falj in a settlement represents a self-sufficient hydrological society, whose members must co-operate, despite deeply rooted differences and tribal enmities which have caused separate fortified quarters with towers and battlements to be built. In Izki for example, there are two adjoining quarters, called Yaman and Nizar -which represent the basic tribal difference in Oman like the divisions between Hināwi and Ghāfiri. The inhabitants of each quarter are historically opposed to each other, but as they are dependant on the same falaj system, are compelled to co-operate. Civil wars - particularly the disastrous wars of the ninth century AD (third century AH) - were responsible for destroying much of the country's falj system, and there is no doubt that much larger areas were under cultivation even in comparatively recent times. But even this larger area would only have been a part of what was cultivated in the sixth century AD.[5]

Behind the coastal plain of Dhofar, in limited areas are frankincense trees, carefully husbanded.

Nearly as many Omanis would traditionally have been fishermen, and the more adventurous have long been the traders of the Indian Ocean. The Gulf of Oman and the Arabian Sea is rich in a wide variety of sea life. Where the Hajar mountains meet the sea, what seem to be completely barren fjords above the water-line, underneath team with life; coral reefs support a whole inter-dependent eco-system of plants, crustaceans, squid and molluscs, as well as a huge range of tropical fish.[6] Great shoals of sardines are sometimes trawled up onto the beach, and after drying, are used both for food and for valuable fertilisers.

Between the farmers and the fishermen, the bedu roam the more barren lands, as across Arabia as a whole. Sometimes after rain in the mountains, large areas of apparently lifeless desert will turn green for a few days in the outwash, and goats and camels will be herded to temporary feeding grounds; these days though, the more valuable camels may be transported in the back of a Toyota pick-up. It must be noted however, that the classical division between city or settled arab ḥaḍar, and nomad badw, is not appropriate to Oman, where all of traditional Omani society is tribal and therefore badw.[7]

Oil was struck only thirty years ago, after thirty years of exploration made difficult by limited political hegonomy. Economic development was strictly limited for ten years; only in the last twenty years has there been rapid growth of urban areas. Now most Omani families will have one or two members working in the Capital. Expatriate workers find their way not only to the urban centres, but also into the loneliest wadis, as farm-labourers as well as teachers and nurses; state education and health-care is available for all.

The old town forts remain, many undergoing careful restoration; they guard the palm-groves,sometimes a long way from the mountains; otherwise, deep among the mountains, watch-towers give away the presence of habitation. The old Sūq or Market has been demolished and rebuilt in many towns; concrete replaces mud, although without the same cooling quality. With an oil industry to protect, modern armament focuses on the airfields of Musandam, Sib, and Maṣīrah; in the south, Thumrait and Ṣalalah guard against the threat of incursion from Yemen. A sizable army builds on the fighting tradition of independent tribes. The fishing and trading history contribute to the Oman navy, with its patrol boats which in the Gulf War of the Eighties, played a significant part in keeping the Straits of Hormuz open; the stories of Sinbad the sailor, are likely to be a composite of many travellers' tales told by returning Omani sailors.[8] A new navy base at Wudam, between Ṣuḥār and Barkah has been recently completed, by moving a huge quanity of rock from behind Rustāq 40k. away, to construct the harbour wall.

In the last year or so, English-speaking guides have been appointed to the larger forts. Tourism, although carefully controlled, is being developed. Only thirty years ago, a general guide to Oman could speak of a total lack of tourism, although anticipating its coming:

> One day there will be afternoon coach trips from Muscat to Fanjah for it is only fifty miles distant, and is a distilled version of all Omani villages; a ford over the wadi, a falaj, date groves, watch-towers

hanging like eagles over a steep village, mountains behind. There will be a restaurant there, and very pleasant too. I used to enjoy watching a string of camels plod very purposefully through the shallow water...[9]

There is now a long cantilevered bridge sweeping the main road to Nizwah high over the old ford. The village itself is abandoned on the side of the mountain, for flatter ground where pumps now drive the water supply. And coach trips, yes, as well as the regular 'bus service to Nizwah, Ṣūr, and Ṣalalah, 900 kilometres away. Such sentiment needs to be balanced with the economic need of a nation which does not have huge known oil reserves - 4.3 billion barrels.[10] A tourism that is sensitive to the customs of the inhabitants could be beneficial to Oman, and as this study will attempt to show, there is much that Oman has to teach the wider world.

NOTES AND REFERENCES:

1. HAWLEY, Donald, 1989, Oman and its Renaissance, Stacey International, London, (revised edition) p.54
2. National Geographic Society, January 1991, Map of the Middle East.
3. CARTER, J.R.L., 1982, Tribes in Oman, Peninsular Pub., London, p.10
4. WILKINSON, J.C., 1987, The Imāmate tradition of Oman, Cambridge University Press, p.101
5. HAWLEY, D., Oman and its Renaissance, op. cit. p.132. Other detail about fuluj and their operation can be found in: J. C. WILKINSON, in Journal of Oman Studies, and in The Imāmate tradition of Oman, op. cit., pp. 23-5
6. BOSCH, Dr Donald and Mrs Eloise, (medical missionaries in Oman, have published several books on the subject of the sea-life of Oman, including:) Sea-shells of Oman, 1973, Longmans, London and New York. Also, Sea-Shells of Southern Arabia, 1989, Motivate Publishing, United Arab Emirates.
7. WILKINSON, J.C., The Imāmate tradition of Oman, op. cit. p94
8. SEVERIN, Tim, 1982, The Sinbad Voyage, Hutchinson and Co., London, p17
9. SKEET, Ian, 1985, Oman before 1970, the end of an era, Faber and Faber, London, 1985, p. 212 (First published 1974, as Muscat and Oman, the end of an era)
10. National Geographic Society Map of the Middle East, January 1991.

2. An early history of Ibāḍism:

The Ibāḍī are named after ᶜAbdullāh bin Ibāḍ,of Basrah. He was a disciple of Abu'l Shaᶜtha' Jābir bin Zayd al-Azdī, from Oman; how Jābir learned of Islām, is uncertain. There are various stories of how news of Muḥammad first reached the settlements either side of the Hajar. There is the story of Māzin bin Ghaḍūbah, who came from the town of Samail. He had been guarding his idol Najir, worshipped by Banī Khatoma and Banī Al-Samit tribes in Samail, when one day he heard a voice from behind the idol, telling him of the Prophet sent among the Arabs and telling him to trust him. Then a man came from the al-Ḥijāz, and was asked: 'what is the news?' He said: 'A man called Aḥmad has appeared and tells everyone: Accept the call of God.' So Māzin crushed his idol and went to the Prophet of God. The Prophet prays for Oman: 'guide the people and make them firm'. 'More!' says Māzin. 'the sea to be bountiful, no enemy over them from those not among them.' Māzin's life changed, he had only four wives, and a son called Hiyari bin Māzin. Oman became a fertile land and had good fishing.[1]

It was as if Māzin wanted to say for the Omanis: 'The new religion was welcome and would be adopted, but please could economic benefits and political independence also be safeguarded?' The blessing granted by the Prophet is a kind of theological and political recognition of the Omani request; if Omanis are to consent to any rule, it will have to be internally accepted, and not imposed by external domination. Whether this particular narrative is authentic in every detail, or only in general, it still summarises clearly and precisely the expectations of the Omanis from their new religion. Moreover, since the time of al-ᶜAwtabī (5th/11th century), it has been taken for granted that the status in which Omanis live, has been granted to them by no less than the Prophet himself. The battles that were fought, and the political and economic consequences that followed, are to be explained from this deeply religious standpoint.[2]

The records are more reliable, and without necessarily contradicting the story of Māzin, that ᶜAmr bin al-ᶜĀṣ, a merchant from Makkah, of the prophet's tribe the Quraish, was sent by Muḥammad to consolidate Islām in Oman. The main tribes were al-Azd and ᶜĀdnān, under the leadership of King Julandy and then his sons, princes Jayfar and ᶜAbd. ᶜAmr was later to become the governor of Egypt, and a large mosque was built in Cairo in his honour; but no similar memorial exists in Oman.[3]

The text of the letter, said to be from the Prophet, which ᶜAmr carried to Oman, is (after the Bismillah):

> Peace be upon those who follow the true religion. After compliments,
> I call you to embrace Islām - accept it and you will be saved, for I am

> the messenger of God to all humanity. (I have come) to warn the living that affliction will befall unbelievers. If you accept Islām, as I hope you will, all will be well, but if you refuse to accept it, your kingdom will vanish and my horses will trample your grounds and my religion will triumph over your kingdom.' The letter was stamped with the seal of the prophet which read: There is no God but Allah and Muḥammad is the Messenger of Allah.[4]

Did the people of Oman accept Islām out of conviction or fear, strategy or expediency? Ibāḍī sympathisers will quote King Solomon's letter to Bilqis, Queen of Sheba - in the Qur'ān, Sūrah 27: 27-31 as an example of how it was a conversion of conviction.[5] But it was also strategy: invited by formal letter to become a follower of Islām, and when the no-doubt-expected refusal was received, the Persian governor of Rustāq on the eastern side of the mountains was besieged by the Azd princes, ᶜAbd and his brother. They expelled him, and then the main Persian garrison at Ṣuḥār. Thus the Arab Azdi's took possession of settled lands, so laboriously developed by the Persians, with their water-channel, or falj systems, at the foot of the Hajar mountains.:

> The Persians were obliged to leave all the gold, silver and weaponry they had. Their properties were taken as ṣawāfī (state) domains.[6]

Some kind of redistribution of wealth took place resulting from the new Islāmic egalitarian principles, so adding to the affluence felt by the common populace. Muḥammad Ibn Saᶜd (168-230 AH/ 784-845 AD) mentions that ᶜAmr bin al-ᶜĀṣ took alms from the rich people, and distributed them among the poor people.[7]

ᶜAmr bin al-ᶜĀṣ remained in Oman for two years until the death of the Prophet. He then returned to Makkah, with ᶜAbd, one of the Azdi princes. Caliph Sayyadina Abū Bakr welcomed prince ᶜAbd with his accompanying Azd nobility to Medinah; good relations remained, except for a case of trouble over taxes. During ᶜUmar's caliphate, Oman was under the Governorship of ᶜUthman bin al-ᶜĀṣ al Thaqāfī, who had his Headquarters in Bahrain. ᶜAbd bin Julandy died, and his brother Jayfar in 634 AD/ 13 AH. ᶜAbd's son then ruled Oman, into the Caliphates of ᶜUthmān and ᶜAlī.

There is one other strand from the early stories that is important to the Ibāḍī.... Not far from Jabal Akhḍar, on the western side, the city of Nizwah draws its water, from wells and falj. South and west of Nizwah lie desert, such as Rubᶜ al-Khālī, the Empty Quarter; it thus made a good centre for defence. Near to the ancient city, is the palm-grove of Firq; behind the village, outcrops of the mountains loom, steeples of rock; despite little rain, cloud often hides the peaks, particularly in the early morning. I was there one dawn; for those sensitive to the numinous, this is surely one of Islām's holy places. About the year 18 after the Hijrah, Abu'l Shaᶜtha'

Jābir bin Zayd al-Azdī, was born at Firq.[8] He was to be called the 'rock foundation' of Ibāḍism.[9] During the time of the third of the caliphs - ᶜUthmān - after the Prophet, Jābir left Nizwah, and journeyed to Basrah to learn more of Islām.

There, it is said, Jābir met with some of the Prophet's companions, including ᶜĀ'ishah, the Prophet's wife, and was acquainted with seventy of those who had been at the battle of Badr. He became a friend of Ḥasan al-Baṣrī, the Muftī of Basrah, and around them formed a group - which included Muslims from North Africa - to be eventually named after the contemporary of Jābir, ᶜAbdullāh bin Ibāḍ. It is Jābir however, who is reckoned in Oman as the main source of Ibāḍī teachings, 'considered by Sunnī and Ibāḍī, as a most learned Muslim, of equal eminence with the Muftī.'[10]

From the companions of the Prophet, Jābir was probably the earliest collector of traditions. His original work was called the Diwān, and consisted of five parts; but it is now lost, 'the only copy of it was found in about the 3rd/9th century in the library of the ᶜAbbāsids at Baghdad.[11] His followers it seems, also recorded these aḥādīth, which appear in the Ibāḍī 'foundation' document, the Jāmiᶜ al-Saḥīḥ or Thulāthiyāt, together with sayings of Abū ᶜUbaydah and ᶜAbdullāh bin Abbās.[12]

The early Ibāḍī distinctiveness centred around the concept of the pure Islāmic state which they believed existed in the time of the first Caliphs Abū Bakr (632-634 AD/ 11-13 AH) and ᶜUmar (634-44 AD/ 13-23 AH), before it came to be corrupted believe in the time of ᶜUthmān (644-56 AD/ 23-35 AH). Their claim is that they developed a true legal system that was earlier and more authentic than that of the four orthodox schools.[13] Those who do not regard the movement as a true return to fundamentals, rather one of the various Khawārij, or 'outsiders' sects, would probably impute the lower motive of grabbing the main chance, in terms of power both in Basrah, and in their homelands. Either way, Ibāḍī doctrine came to be tested, in the troubles that then enveloped Islām.

The story of division in the house of Islām has been told from many perspectives.

> Salīl bin Razik begins his history: 'The most learned and accurate historians agree in this, that whereas after the disturbances and dissensions which had occurred among the people, the supreme authority was eventually vested in Muᶜāwīyah...' The translator G.P. Badger adds a footnote: The reference here is to the differences among the Mussulmans which led to the assassination of ᶜUthmān, the election of ᶜAlī and his subsequent deposition, and the accession of his son Ḥasan, who eventually resigned the Khalifate, in favour of

Muᶜāwīyah. A succinct account of these intestine feuds, chiefly from original sources, is found in the Modern Universal History, vol. i...[14]

From an Ibāḍī perspective: Caliph ᶜUthmān had been charged with nepotism by 'Amr, Governor of Egypt; ᶜUthmān retaliated by appointing a new Egyptian Governor. The Egyptian people saw fit to support 'Amr, and a group marched to Medinah in 656 AD/ 35 AH, to kill ᶜUthmān. Then followed the dispute between ᶜAlī, Ḥasan, Ḥussain, and Muᶜāwīyah.

The question is raised, was there any specific Omani role in the First Civil War? Were there any early incidents that might explain some of the major attitudes of options followed by the Omanis later on? One of the major criticisms against ᶜUthmān was that:

> ...he prevented the people of al-Bahrayn and ᶜUman from selling their food until food of alms was sold...[15]

Al-Khirrīt bin Rāshid al-Sāmī (d. 38 AH/ 658 AD) at the head of three hundred Banū Nājiyah was with ᶜAlī in the battle of Ṣafīn. After al-taḥkīm the arbitration, a series of theological and military confrontations began, which led to the killing of al-Khirrīt and some of the Banū Nājiyah, as well as the enslavement of five hundred members of the tribe, who after being Muslims, had reverted to Christianity during the turmoil. This is further explored, in Early Islāmic Oman and Early Ibāḍism in the Arabic Sources, a Cambridge Ph.D. thesis, by Aḥmad ᶜUbaydlī.[16]

The struggle lasted five years, and ended for ᶜAlī when he was attacked as he entered a mosque - he died a few days later. A further nine months passed, while the shīᶜat-ᶜAlī, the party of ᶜAlī, tried to rally their forces against Muᶜāwīyah; but, with an army of 60,000, Muᶜāwīyah persuaded his opponents (with an army of only 40,000) at Ṣafīn, to accept what seemed at first like a compromise, but turned out to be capitulation to him (AD 657/ 36 AH). The battle had lasted for weeks - but on it's most decisive day, Muᶜāwīyah had his warriors put pages of the Qur'ān on their lances, thus indicating his desire to decide their differences on the basis of the Qur'ān. ᶜAlī reluctantly agreed, setting up two generals, one from each side, to arbitrate. A group of ᶜAlī's soldiers, mainly of the tribe of Tamīm, saw this as elevating the decision of men over that of God and withdrew to a nearby village to protest. Here they elected a fellow soldier, ᶜAbdullāh bin Waḥb al-Rasibī as their leader. It was this move which gave the group it's name, Khawārij, that is to say, the 'seceders'.

When the arbitration went in favour of Muᶜāwīyah, many more soldiers joined the Khārijite cause, thus causing a radical opposition force which promptly rejected ᶜAlī's claim to the caliphate and branded everyone who did not agree with them, as apostates from the true faith. ᶜAlī was forced to move against them, and killed most of them in an attack on their main camp, but their survivors continued on as a guerilla force; it could be said that they have harassed the main body of Muslims ever since. In 661 AD/ 41 AH, one of their number killed ᶜAlī in revenge for the death of his wife's family. Muᶜawīyah became the fifth Caliph, and began a family dynasty for the Sunnī group within Islām. The party of ᶜAlī proclaimed his son Ḥasan as Caliph; he abdicated in favour of his brother Hussain who was violently murdered, on the 10th of the month Muḥarram - a date very special since then to the Shīᶜites.

Many Ibāḍī do not consider themselves to be among the Khawārij. Rather, they would regard groups such as the Azāriqah in the first century (A.H.), 'known for their violence in resolution of disputes, for fanaticism and murder of defenceless people' as Khawārij.:

> Of all these movements, the most dangerous to the unity of the Muslim Empire and the most terrible on account of its ferociously uncompromising character was without doubt led by Nāfiᶜ bin al-Azrakh which gave the Khawārij temporary control of Kirmān, Fārs and other eastern provinces...[17]

Some Ibāḍī I have spoken to, would regard those who follow the more recent Wahhābī movement as Khawārij, while acknowledging that they, in return, are regarded as Khawārij. The Ṣufriyyah were less 'extremist'; they originate from a split between Nāfiᶜ bin al-Azrakh and his colleague the Tamīmī ᶜAbdullāh bin al-Ṣaffār, on the issue of istiᶜrāḍ (the murder of adversaries and their familes).[18] Like the Ibāḍī, al-Ṣaffār and his followers preferred to work for peaceful reform within the Muslim community; their position was, to accept the possibility of revolt only if a ruler was clearly unjust. Although the Ibāḍī draw clear distinctions here, denying being 'part and parcel' of the Khawārij, they have usually been classed with the Khawārij by everyone but themselves. The fact is not disputed, that Jābir and his followers, including ᶜAbd Allāh bin Ibāḍ, were among those who did not want to compromise with Muᶜawīyah. But, as their doctrines developed to be so largely peaceable in terms of living alongside others, standing (with a few violent exceptions) for tolerance, if they are to be classed with the Khawārij, at least it should be with some qualification.[19]

As the one after whom the Ibāḍī are named, ᶜAbdullāh bin Ibāḍ is described by Sheikh Aḥmed Hamoud Al-Maamiry:

> He was a great teacher and a staunch Muslim who would not compromise his faith or allow himself to be lured by worldly attractions. His belief was unshakable and he knew no fear except his fear of God, and would not hesitate to speak the truth or reprimand when necessary...

cAbdullāh bin Ibāḍ received a letter from cAbdul Malik bin Marwan in which he sought his opinion with regard to the then prevailing events and those which took place previously, and in reply, he wrote his famous letter of reproach explaining to him the mistakes which have been made by religious leaders after the death of Caliph Omar which caused divisions among the Muslims into various groups and sects....

Among other things cAbdullāh wrote in his letter to Marwan is the following:

> ...In what you dispute about the Book of God, its judgement is with God; that is God my Master - on Him I trust and to Him I lean, and this is the clear path that God has guided before us, Muḥammad - Peace be upon him - and the two appropriate Caliphs after him. So whoever follows him does not go astray and whoever abandons him does not receive guidance.[20]

Success had marked the beginning of their development. Mucāwīyah appointed a Governor of Basrah who was sympathetic to the Ibāḍī; re-organising the city into akhmās (fifths), the Ibāḍī Azdī's were given considerable responsibility. More Azdī's arrived in Basrah to share in power. Their leader al Muhallab bin abi Ṣufra gained control of the city so effectively that it became known as Basrah al Muhallab. 3,000 Azdī's fought in his army against the Khawārij. The Ibāḍī understanding of Islām had gained support from those who were too powerful politically (the Qacad the quietists[21]), to risk losing power by behaving like the Khawārij. However, when Muhallab died 702 AD/ 82 AH, their fortunes took a turn for the worse. cAbdul Malik bin Marwan became the first of the Ummayyad caliphs, and mistrusted the Ibāḍī of Basrah. Jābir and his friends attempted a debate with him, as to the nature of the state of Islām, but they failed to reach agreement. The new governor of Iraq appointed by cAbdul Malik, Al Hajjāj bin Yūsif, set out to destroy the power of the Ibāḍī; Ummayyad rule was to have no opposition. Facing persecution, Jābir chose the way of passive opposition, and continued his leadership in secret; but finally, he withdrew from Basrah, returning to Nizwah; others returned to North Africa.

Al Hajjāj had imprisoned one of Jābir's followers, the blind and poor Abū cUbaydah Muslim bin Abi Karīma Al-Tamīmy, with another follower, Zamām bin al-Saib. Despite alleged atttempts to kill them with a diet of only oil and maize, Abū cUbaydah survived (with the help of his friends smuggling food to them), and he came to have wide significance, as a strategist for the Ibāḍī.

The concept of kitmān - where the state of Islām did not have to have a visible leader - began in Basrah. An Ibāḍī shares with the Kharāwij, if nothing else, the doctrine of election for the Imām; if no-one is suitable, or if it is politicaly expedient not to elect an Imām, then kitman allows this state of affairs.

Ahmad ᶜUbaydlī presents a convincing argument for the Ibāḍī understanding of kitmān as being the reason behind the confusion as to who the real founder of Ibāḍism was. He suggests that the actual leadership of Jābir was intentionally hidden, behind the naming of the group after one of Jābir's disciples, namely ᶜAbdullāh bin Ibāḍ.

> It appears that some conscious decision must have been made that the real leader was to be highly educated but to be kept in secrecy and far away from the daily affairs of the movement while yet in full control. Another person was to be the public leader of the movement, who was to be strong from the military point of view and able to secure the public leadership and image of the movement. However, he was to follow sincerely the commands of the real leader.[22]

(see Chapters ten and eleven on possible implications of the doctrine of kitmān in dialogue today). The present Grand Muftī of Oman says of that period, and of the ᶜAbbāsid rule that followed:

> many tongues shouted against them.... despite tyrannical rule which digressed from the correct system of Islām....[23]

Some Ibāḍī fled to their fastness of the Hajar mountains, and fought off their attackers at first successfully. Then, with an army of 40,000 conscripted from the Azdī's natural enemies, Al Ḥujaj master-minded a determined attack. It was launched with two prongs, one on the Bāṭinah coast, the other from on the west side of Ras Musandam. This proved too much for the Azdī leaders, who fled to exile, some to East Africa. A period of kitmān followed. A revolt in Basrah, 720 AD/ 102 AH, proved unsuccessful, many Azdī troops dying in battle. The words of the song of the victorious enemies of the Ibāḍī are recorded:

> The fires of Al Mazun (a sneering reference to the persianised Omanis) and its peoples are extinguished. They sought to kindle a revolt, but you have left no standard for them to follow nor any soldier to al Muhallab's people.[24]

Back in Basrah, on the death of Al Ḥujaj, Abū ᶜUbaydah was released from prison, on condition that 'he did not teach a single letter.' Establishing himself as a basket-weaver in a basement, Abū ᶜUbaydah taught many people:

> From Oman: Imām Al-Shary Abū Hamza, Imām Al-Rabii bin Ḥabib author of Al-Musnād al-Saḥiḥ, Imām Al-Julandy bin Masoud; from Qarasan: Hashim bin ᶜAbdullāh al-Qarasāny; from al-Hijaz: Muḥammad bin ᶜAbbas al-Madāny; from Egypt: Muḥammad bin

ᶜAbd al-Masry; from Iraq: Abi Ghassān Bakry bin ᶜUmrū; from the Yemen: Imām Talib Al-Ḥaq, known as ᶜAbdullāh bin Yahyā al-Kindy.[25]

Also from the Yemen, came Abū Sagaaf al-Muasīry al-Yamany.[26]

A watchman would give the alarm by pulling a chain if anyone approached who was not among them, and they would stop lessons and begin to make baskets. Confined in his basement, Abū ᶜUbaydah watched world events, and through his students, began to influence them in a remarkable way. The Ibāḍī were becoming an active political movement, believing themselves to understand better than other Muslims their daᶜwah[27] - their 'call' from God, and the 'call' which they offer on behalf of God: to believe in the true religion, Islām.

In the next chapter, the development of the Ibāḍī in North Africa and South Arabia will be considered. It is perhaps salutary to conclude this chapter with a 'balancing view' (but not necessarily a conclusive one) from J. C. Wilkinson, The Imāmate tradition of Oman, one of the sources for this chapter:

> The fact is that the origins and development of Ibāḍism were much more rough and ready than appears in the standard madhhab (school of doctrine) and its history, elaborated over more than a millennium. The reality is that Jabir bin Zayd is hardly ever referred to by the early jurists of Oman, and that his collection of aḥādīth is probably spurious, largely the work of A. Ya'qub al-Warjlāni in the sixth/twelth century; that his successor A. ᶜUbaydah could never have been a proper pupil of Jābir's..... But, what matters for understanding the inner view of Ibāḍism and Imāmate legitimacy is the image of the early development of Ibāḍism .....[28]

Notes and References:

1. MAAMIRY, Ahmed H. Al-, 1989 (revised edition), Oman and Ibāḍhism, Lancers Books,New Delhi, pp. 6-8 (drawing from al-ᶜAwtabī, I:257 - 5th/ 11th Century).
2. ᶜUBAYDLĪ, Aḥmad, 1989, Early Islāmic Oman and Early Ibāḍism in the Arabic Sources, Cambridge Ph.D. Thesis, p. 41
3. HAWLEY, Donald, 1989 (revised edition), Oman and it's Renaissance, Stacey International, London, p.166
4. MAAMIRY, Ahmed H. Al-, Oman and Ibādhism, op. cit. p.9
5. KHALĪLĪ, Ahmed H. Al-, 1986, Who are the Ibādhis?, translated by A.H.Al-Maamiry, Oman

6. LØKKEGAARD, F, 1950, Islāmic taxation in the Classic period, Copenhagan, p. 49
7. ^{c}UBAYDLĪ, Ahmad, Early Islamic Oman and Early Ibāḍism, op. cit., p. 40
8. EI^{2}, Vol III p.649
9. MAAMIRY, A. H. Al-, Oman and Ibādhism, op. cit. p.28
10. HAWLEY, Donald, Oman and it's Renaissance, op. cit. p.167
11. EI^{2}, Vol. III p.649
12. MAAMIRY, A. H. Al-, Oman and Ibādhism, op. cit. p.30
13. KHALĪLĪ, A. H. Al-, Who are the Ibādhi? op. cit.
14. RAZIK, S., 1871, History of the Imāms and Seyyids of Oman, translated and edited by G. P. Badger, London, (new impression 1986, Darf Publishers, London) p.1
15. ^{c}UBAYDLĪ, Aḥmad, Early Islāmic Oman and Early Ibāḍism, op. cit., p.45
16. ibid. p. 45
17. EI^{2}, Vol. IV, p. 1075
18. EI^{1}, Vol. IV (part 1), p. 498, and EI^{2}, Vol. I, p. 810
19. MAAMIRY, A. H. Al-, Oman and Ibādhism, op. cit. p.42
20. ibid, pp. 31-2
21. EI^{2}, Vol. III p.648
22. ^{c}UBAYDLĪ, Aḥmad, Early Islāmic Oman and Early Ibāḍism, op. cit., p. 53/4
23. KHALĪLĪ, A. H. Al-, Who are the Ibādhi? op. cit.
24. WILKINSON, J. C.,1972, 'Origins of the Omani State' in The Arabian Peninsular, Society and Politics. Edited by D. Hopwood, London George Allen and Unwin, p.74
25 EI^{2}, Vol. III p.651
26. KHALĪLĪ, A. H. Al-, 1989, The Spread of Ibādhism in Northern Africa, Oman, p.9
27. EI^{2}, Vol. II pp. 168-171
28. WILKINSON, J.C. The Imāmate tradition of Oman op. cit. p. 153

3. Ibāḍism in North Africa and South Arabia.

Abū ᶜUbaydah sent his student Salāmah bin Saᶜd (722-3 AD/ 104 AH) to the Maghrib[1], after he had learned while on the ḥajj:

> ...of the oppressions of the Umayyad Caliphs... to teach that Islām is represented by the example of the prophet and his orthodox Caliphs, and is not represented by the example of the Banī Umayyad who brought the rule devoid of Islām.[2]

So began his mission from Sirt on the Libyan coast, continuing to Western Algeria; it was consolidated under the leadership of Imām Al-Ḥarith bin Tāliyd al-Ḥaḍrāmi, and his General ᶜAbd al-Jabbār.

But the Umayyad agent ᶜAbd al-Raḥmān bin Ḥabīb from Qayrawān (near Tripoli) sent people purporting to discuss with the leaders, but in fact to kill them. A letter was sent to Abū ᶜUbaydah, who counselled caution, until ᶜAbd al-Raḥmān could be exposed. Salāmah bin Saᶜd continued his mission across North Africa. Four students of his are remembered by the Ibāḍī historians:

> From Libya, Ismāᶜīl bin Darrar al-Ghadamīsy; from Algeria, ᶜĀṣim al-Sadrati; from Tunis, Abū Dāwud al-Qibilī al-Nafzawa; and ᶜAbdul Raḥmān bin Rustam.[3]

ᶜAbdul Raḥmān bin Rustam came from Qayrawān, but was originally from Iran; as a child he had gone on ḥajj where his father died, then his mother's hand was asked for by a man from Qayrawān. Impressed by the teaching of Salāmah bin Saᶜd, he returned to Basrah (752-3 AD/ 135 AH) to learn about his father, but:

> When he entered the basement where the great teacher Abū ᶜUbaydah was teaching, he forgot all his aspirations and began to concentrate on preaching the word of God. Never thinking of his father's belongings or of a home, he believed that the home of the Muslim is where he can fulfil his religious obligations and teach the word of God.[4]

Imām ᶜAbdul Ḥamid bin Maghtīr al-Nafusy had already come from Jabal Nafūsah to Abū ᶜUbaydah. he returned home, and taught there until as an old man, Imām ᶜAbd al-Wahhāb, the successor of ᶜAbdul Raḥmān bin Rustam came there.

From Yemen, Imām ᶜAbu'l-Khattāb al-Muafīry al-Yamany joined the four from North Africa. Abū ᶜUbaydah appointed him the leader; knowing that tribal favouritism would prevent the spread of Ibāḍī teachings, he saw the advantage of putting the North Africans under an Imām who was from the Yemen. By this time, the Umayyad Caliphate had been replaced by the ᶜAbbāsid dynasty, 'who were no less in oppression, arrogance and tyranny.' [5] The four, having pledged themselves to ᶜAbu'l-Khattāb as Imām, went to the ᶜAbbāsid governor of Tripoli and gave him the option of joining them, or leaving. Choosing the latter, he was even given enough food and weapons to defend himself with until he arrived in Egypt 'proving the magnaminity of the Ibāḍī even in war.' [6] There is a story of the war undertaken against Qayrawān's unjust ᶜAbbāsid rulers, when the dead Warsajūna soldiers were left lying with their arms intact, and a passing woman gave the battle it's name: the battle of sleep - riqāda.[7] ᶜAbdul Raḥmān bin Rustam was appointed Imām of Qayrawān.

Under the ᶜAbbāsid Caliph Al-Manṣūr, Muḥammad bin al-Ashᶜath al Khuzāᶜī, the governor of Egypt, was sent to overthrow ᶜAbu'l-Khattāb. he attempted this by appearing to retreat before ᶜAbu'l-Khattāb's army, which then went home for harvesting. Then the ᶜAbbāsid army counter attacked and at Tawārgha many Ibāḍiyyah were slaughtered. The Imām of Qayrawān made to help ᶜAbu'l-Khattāb; on hearing he was dead tried to return to Qayrawān only to find the people had revolted and had followed Omar bin ᶜUthmān al-Quraishy, so he resorted to the high Atlas mountains.

After ᶜAbu'l-Khattāb's death the Ibāḍiyyah remnant retreated into the interior of Tripolitania or crossed into the central Maghrib. Raḥmān bin Rustam rebuilt the town of Tāhirt (inland from what is now Algiers). Centred there, Ibāḍī influence grew again. The ᶜAbbāsid governor sent to sort out the Ibāḍiyyah made a good start, defeating Raḥmān bin Rustam in battle, but was then killed in a skirmish at Qayrawān, 771 AD/ 154 AH.[8] This time, Ibāḍī authority was unchallenged over a wide area, possibly even as far as the Ibāḍiyyah of Oman. A temporary peace was made with both the ᶜAbbāsids and the Aghlabids, a dynasty which ruled over a territory which included much of modern Tunisia, largely independant from the ᶜAbbāsids.

Delegations were sent to West Africa, 'in Ghana and Mali many became Ibāḍī Muslims... and until now are referred to as a good example in straightness and honesty...' [9] The story is told how Ibāḍī muslims came from the east with aid and found the Imām working in the mud with the builders:

> Such Imām never wanted positions, corruption, no comfort for themselves but were toiling for the sake of the comfort of the people. They used to go naked in order to clothe their people and to go hungry in order to feed their people. Thus, their caliphate was tantamount to the orthodox caliphate which the Prophet (S.A.W.) left for his companions. That was how the Ibāḍiyyah spread in North Africa. After ᶜAbdul Raḥmān bin Rustam, his son ᶜAbd al-Wahhāb was elected, and the dynasty continued for more than 1½ centuries. The whole period was known as the period of justice and was famous for its straightness. Non - Ibāḍī authors have written about that period

and until today Algeria is proud of that Rustamid state which prevailed in its soil and which was known for its justice, love and fairness.[10]

The town of Tāhirt had become by the second half of the 8th century AD (2nd Century AH), the centre for intensive trade south across the Sahara; during the reign of Imām Aflāh bin ᶜAbd al-Wahhāb (823-71 AD/ 208-58 AH) there was even an Ibāḍī ambassador at the court of the king of Ghana or of Gao.[11] But for North African Ibāḍiyyah, the best was soon over. In 839 AD/ 224 AH, as a result of attacks by Ibāḍī tribesmen, the Aghlabids divided the Ibāḍī territory in two. The now weakened Tahirt Imāmate continued until 909 AD/ 296 AH when it was conquered by the armies of Abu ᶜAbdullāh al-Shīᶜī, who established on the ruins of the Rustamid and Aghlabid states, the new and powerful Fātimid kingdom.[12] The last Imām, Abū Yūsuf Yaᶜkūb fled 250 miles south to the oasis of Wargla. Several attempts were made to reassert Ibāḍī power, but they all ended in failure.

In the 11th and 12th centuries AD/ 3rd and 4th centuries AH, five centres in the region of Mzab (Algeria) were active in keeping the Ibāḍī flame burning, and in the seventeenth century there were seven towns governed by a common religious council - al-ᶜazzābah. In 1835 AD/ 1251 AH the area became a French protectorate, and in 1882 AD/ 1299 AH was annexed to Algeria. Today in North Africa, Ibāḍiyyah are to be found in: the Mzab (Algeria), on Jerba Island (Tunisia), and in the Jabal Nafūsah (Libya). The Libyan group did try to establish an Imāmate in defiance of Italian rule in 1911 AD/ 1329 AH but without success.

One consequence of the fall of the Tāhirt Imāmate, was the destruction of the Maᶜṣūmah library there, burnt by Abū ᶜAbdullāh al Shīᶜī in 909 AD/ 297 AH.[13] Another library, of Qaṣr Wallam was also lost at Jabal Nafūsah. It was common practice during Muslim wars to destroy the literature of dissidents and it was for this reason that the Ibāḍiyyah lost their books.[14] Those that survived were often hidden, and sometimes no doubt forgotten as their custodian died. But, some collections did survive.

In the library of Sheikh Yūsuf Muḥammad al-Bārūnī of Al-Ḥashshān, Jerba, 32 leaves (pages) were discovered (in old Maghribī hand), undated, but perhaps 6th century A.H., containing 18 letters from Jābir bin Zaid, to his friends and followers. These are the earliest extant Ibāḍī documents, 'this correspondence should show some light on his life.' [15] Other material for which it is claimed also derives from Jābir, was part of a Kitāb al-Nikāḥ, (dated 1797 AD/ 1211 AH) containing legal opinions on marriage in the early period of Islam.

Another treatise, Risālah fī al-zakāt (dated 1797 AD/ 1211 AH) in the same collection is designated as from Abū ᶜUbaydah, Jābir's successor, addressed to

Ismācīl bin Sulaimān al-Maghribī (previously unknown) containing legal opinions; such are to be found throughout Ibāḍī writings, but this collection explains some of his organisational ideas relating to the taxation zakāt system, showing how Ibāḍī society was trying to establish itself.[16]

From Abū cUbaydah's secret centre of learning in Basrah, students who had come to him for teaching were sent also to the Ḥaḍramawt.[17] His pupil Ṭālib al-Ḥaqq cAbdullāh bin Yaḥyā al-Kindy went to Ḥaḍramawt with Biljī bin Aqbah al-Uzdy from the Bāṭinah coast of Oman; there he was 'unanimously chosen' as Imām, and gave the Umayyad governor the option of joining him or leaving; he left for Ṣancā'. (Another example of Ibāḍī moderation?). The Umayyad agent in Ṣanacā' organised an army of 30,000 fighters (Ibāḍī statistic!) which was beseiged by 1600 of the Ibāḍiyyah.

> They sold their lives for the sake of God... were pursuing on one horse, sharing one blanket, but this poverty did not incite them to take advantage of collecting wealth by stealing. They only wanted God's pleasure.[18]

On taking Ṣancā' and finding the wealth the Umayyads had taken from the people, Ṭālib al-Ḥaqq gave it all back.

After settling in Ṣancā(746 AD/ 129 AH), he sent Abū Ḥamza al-Mukhtār with 700, to Heggaz to link up with some Ibāḍiyyah there under the leadership of Imām Abū al-Ḥūrr Alī bin al-Ḥasān who had his fortunes in Iraq, but:

> When his revenues reached him, he would divide them into half, giving half as alms, then dividing the remaining half, he gave half to meet the requirements of the Muslims, keeping only the balance for himself, his family and his guests.[19]

The Umayyads put him in prison, together with some Shīcī in Makkah where they suffered abuse, but the people forced the soldiers to let them go. This was at the same time as Abū Ḥamza arrived in Makkah with an army of only 900 to 1,000, but without a fight the city surrendered to him. A battle did ensue with the city of Medinah in which Abū Ḥamza was victorious. The Ibāḍiyyah thus became an immediate threat to the Umayyads, centred in Syria, and Marwān bin Muḥammad sent an army under the command of cAbd al-Malik bin cAṭīyyah al-Sacdi to the Holy Cities. Meanwhile, when Abū Ḥamza came to the pulpit of the prophet he defended his people in words that have been preserved in khuṭbas:[20]

> He placed his face where the Prophet used to place his feet. He wept for a long time and then said grumbling: 'How many feet have violated God, abused his sanctity, prevailed on his servants, ruled contrary to the law of God and introducing what the prophet had not known.[21]

Ascending one step of the pulpit he made a speech, beginning by praising God and praying for the prophet.[22] But, after insults were hurled by a soldier, fighting broke out in which Abū Ḥamza was killed. Ibāḍī narratives tell of his body with others being crucified. The Ibāḍī occupation of the Holy Cities was soon over, presumably on arrival of ᶜAbd al-Malik's army. Abū Ḥamza's body remained in public view:

> ...until the 'Umayyids (sic) were overthrown... thus underlining the corruption of the 'Umayyids as against the moderateness of the Ibāḍiyyah. Among those who ride the camel of Banī 'Umayya in our age is a writer who wrote a commentary on the Omani author who mentioned Abū Ḥamza... claiming that Abū Ḥamza oppressed the Muslims when he occupied the Holy Places and led them away from the Muslim authority. Would that Banī 'Umayya were the Muslim authority! Does Islām know what Bani 'Umayya had done? Who had killed the grandson of the Prophet (S.A.W.) Al-Ḥussain bin Alī?..... Islām is innocent from Banī 'Umayya and from their activities. True Islām is with those who follow the straight path and which does not deviate from the Qur'ān and from the Tradition.[23]

On receiving news of Abū Ḥamza's defeat, Ṭālib al-Ḥaqq came from Ṣanᶜā' to prevent the Syrian army from reaching the Yemen. Total defeat of the Ibāḍī army ensued, and Ṭālib al-Ḥaqq was killed. But, fortunately for the Ibāḍiyyah, the Syrian army was at that point recalled, and a peace treaty enabled the Imāmate of Ḥaḍramawt to continue, subject to the ᶜAbbāsid state. The population of this area paid tithes to the Imām of Oman at about the beginning of the 3rd century; subsequent history is obscure.[24]

Students of Abū ᶜUbaydah are said to have reached India as well as Khurasan, Iran and Central Asia. With the waning power of the Umayyad empire, the influence of Abū ᶜUbaydah's ḥamalat al-ᶜilm were to spread widely. The advent of the ᶜAbbāsids meant that some of the Ibāḍiyyah were able to gain the protection of influential members of the families of the new caliphs. But with the death of Abū ᶜUbaydah, probably in Caliph Abū Jaᶜfar's reign (753-75 AD/ 136-58 AH) the influence of the Basrah Ibāḍī waned, and while some remained there, the main focus of their activity from then on, was eastern Arabia, or Oman.[25]

Abū ᶜUbaydah had encouraged the election of Al-Julandā bin Masᶜūd as Imām in Oman (750 AD/ 132 AH), but the ᶜAbbāsids attacked the embryonic state, being suspicious of it's allegience, and Al-Julandā was killed at Ras-al-Khaimah. It was Caliph Al-Saffāḥ who gave the Ibāḍiyyah their next chance, when he appointed from Basrah a secret Ibāḍī sympathiser as governor of Ṣuḥār, and the Ibāḍiyyah worked to establish themselves firmly. The ᶜAbbāsids did not bother to appoint a governor for the Hajar, and a period of inter-tribal warfare followed. The fact was, it was simply not worth their while; the vast expense and difficulty in mounting military operations in these sparcely populated areas far outweighed any possible benefits in terms of increased taxation.

> Such diversity of country and enormous distances meant that communications were always a problem and journeys from one part of the (ᶜAbbāsid) caliphate to another could take weeks or even months. The caliphs set up an official information service; post stations were maintained on the main roads, where official messengers could pick up new mounts; delivery time was up to three months.[26]

Ibāḍī communications without the resources of a Caliphate would have been less formal that those described above, relying on traders, as they kept in touch, politically and theologically, across Arabia and North Africa; many Ibāḍiyyah were themselves traders.[27] The ḥajj was of course an important.occasion for meeting. At Izki in central Oman, another centre for Ibāḍī influence developed, it seems causing some embarrassment to the main group in Basrah. The murder of one, ᶜAbd al-ᶜAzīz by house-guests, was laid at the door of the Basrah Ibāḍiyyah, and they were condemned for the act by the Caliphate. Climbing back from this low-point, some of the prominent Ibāḍiyyah of Basrah, left to develop their doctrinal base in Iski.

This is one of the events behind the saying found in many histories of Oman and accounts of Ibāḍī belief, 'Knowledge was laid in Medinah, hatched in Basrah, and flew to Oman.' It was in Oman that the fledgling grew strongest; but Ibāḍī knowledge 'flew' by means of their traders, on camel-train or by sea, to Yemen and North Africa as well. AḥmadᶜUbaydlī in his research of Arabic texts, underlines the central role of Basrah in the development of Ibāḍism, quoting al-Kudamī from the late 4th Century AH/ 10th Century AD, al-Darjīnī who died. around 670 AH, 1271 AD, and al-Shammākhī, who died 928 AH, 1521 AD.[28]

In Oman, tribal warfare came to a conclusion, with the election of Al-Wārith bin Kaᶜb al-Kharusī as Imām, in 801 AD/ 185 AH, and this time the Ibāḍī state was secured against its attackers for a century, with the defeat of the Caliph's army at Ṣuḥār. During the rule of Imām Mahana bin Jaifa (840-851 AD/ 226-237AH) a disciplined army of defence, of 10,000 men, was organised and stationed at Nizwah. Despite an ᶜAbbāsid 're-conquest' of Oman in 893 AD/ 280 AH, the Ibāḍī Imāmate continue to exist. It was the first 'Golden Age' of the Ibāḍiyyah.

There were those, however, who did not commit themselves irrevocably to the movement. Further south from the main Hajar ranges, and along the Bāṭinah coast with the influence of maritime trading, there were those tribes whose allegience to the Imām was at best nominal, if not non-existent. And: within the Ibāḍī system as well, there seems to be a 'self-destruct' mechanism, which is taken up in the next chapter.

Notes and References:

1. EI^2, Vol III, p.653 (m).
2. KHALĪLĪ, Aḥmed H. Al-, (1989), The Spread of Ibādhism in Northern Africa, Oman, p.11
3. ibid. p.12
4. ibid. p.13
5. ibid. p.15
6. ibid. p.16.
7. ibid. p.17
8. KENNEDY, Hugh, 1981, The early ᶜAbbāsid Caliphate, Croom Helm, London, 1981, p.191. On p. 188 Kennedy refers to the prosperity of the Ibāḍiyyah in Basrah, who developed a commercial community there prior to the death of ᶜAbdul Malik in 705 AD/ 86 AH. His source is: LEWICKI, T., 1971, The Ibāḍites in Arabia and Africa, in *Cahiers d'Histoire Mondiale,* vol. 13, pp. 58-67
9. KHALĪLĪ, A. H. Al-, The Spread of Ibādhism in Northern Africa, op. cit., p.19
10. ibid. pp. 18-9
11. EI^2, Vol III, op. cit. p.657
12. ibid. p.655
13. ᶜUBAYDLĪ, Aḥmad, 1989, Early Islāmic Oman and Early Ibāḍism in the Arabic Sources, Cambridge Ph.D. Thesis, p. 1
14. ENNAMI, A. K., 1970, in an article A description of new Ibāḍī documents from North Africa in the Journal of Semitic Studies, Vol. 15, No. I, Spring, 1970 p. 63
15. ibid. p.66. (But see comment at the end of chapter two by J.C.Wilkinson about reliability of documents purporting to come from Jābir bin Zaid. Wilkinson may not have read this 1970 article, but has read an unpublished Ph.D. thesis by Ennami called studies on Ibāḍism, University of Cambridge 1971.)
16. ibid. p.68
17. EI^2, Vol III, op. cit. p 650
18. KHALĪLĪ, A. H. Al-, The Spread of Ibādhism in Northern Africa, op. cit. p.21
19. ibid. p.23
20. EI^2, Vol III, op. cit. p.651
21. KHALĪLĪ, A. H. Al-, The Spread of Ibādhism in Northern Africa, op. cit. p.25
22. ibid. p.26

23. ibid. p.28
24. EI^2, Vol III, op. cit. p.652
25. ibid. pp. 650/1
26. KENNEDY, Hugh, The early ᶜAbbāsid Caliphate, op. cit., pp. 31-33
27. ibid. pp. 191-2
28. ᶜUBAYDLĪ, Aḥmad, 1989, Early Islāmic Oman and Early Ibāḍism in the Arabic Sources, op. cit. p. 60, quoting Al-KUDAMĪ, Abū Saīd Muḥammad bin Saᶜīd Muḥammad bin Saᶜīd, (late 4/10), al-Istiqāmah (I- III), Oman 1985; AL-DARJĪNĪ, Abū al- ᶜAbbās Aḥmad bin Saᶜīd, (died c. 670/1271), Kitāb ṭabaqat al-mashāyikh bi'l-maghrib (I-II) ed. Ibrāhīm Ṭallāy, Algeria 1394/1974; and AL-SHAMMĀKHĪ, Abu al- ᶜAbbās bin Aḥmad bin Saᶜīd (d. 928/ 1521), al-Siyar, litho (Qusṭanṭīnah), n.d.

4. Yaᶜribi a'imma and Al Bu Saᶜīdi Sultans, until 1900:

The period of rule of the Yaᶜribi a'imma (Imāms) of the seventeenth century rivals, if it does not surpass, the political power and wealth of the First (Golden Age) Imāmate; but, between the two periods the whole region degenerated into tribal disunity. Many tribal attitudes had been broken down by the first Imāmate, The early a'imma showed a great awareness of the value of a sound commercial atmosphere and the problems of the basic agricultural economy:

> Arabs became villagers, and villagers were incorporated into the tribal structures of the Arabs.[1]

Nizwah had become the 'seat' for the Imām, being on the inland side of Jabal Akhḍar, and in the best position for influence and where necessary control, of the interior tribes; but near enough to Rustāq under the mountains on the coastal side, for a fast communication link between them.

The tracks are still there. From a distance, they make quite impossible ascents up many thousands of feet of mountain. But, with careful engineering, and with interminable steps, sometimes cut into the rock, they make safe routes, and fast ones, for those fitter than the average twentieth century westerner. They may have originally been engineered by the first (Persian) settlers two thousand years before, at the same time as the first fulūj.[2] To be kept in use though, such routes need constant maintenance, as sections get easily washed away; perhaps soon only the steps will remain.

I managed one such ascent with some fit military men, from the end of wādī Sahṭan south of Rustāq, two kilometres east of Jabal Shams (3009 metres high). I needed many rests in the heat on the way up, and finally to reach the 'rest and be thankful' ruins of the old mosque (Bait Ma'illat) at the top felt like achievement indeed. But some of the pauses were spent admiring the incredible stone-work of the track, connecting one side of the Hajar to the other, where parapets had not been eroded away, or where steps had been carved into the rock-face of the mountain.

It was more influence than control that kept the state together. Military forces under the direct command of the Imām were small; it was the oath of obedience by the tribes to the Imām that counted, and a continuing desire to live in peace. A delicate balance had to be maintained between the Yaḥmad, the most powerful Azd clan, from which the Imām came generally to be chosen, while the nominating clan„ were the Banī Sāmah. But, as convincingly argued by J. C. Wilkinson:

> ... as wealth and prosperity increase, so the religious ideal weakens; leadership becomes the prerogative of a single group and degenerates

> into temporal power saltānah. The pattern has been repeated several times in Oman's history. There ensues a struggle for power in which tribal solidarity ᶜasabiyah is brought into play, and every potential weakness in the country exploited until full-scale civil war is the outcome. The situation is usually resolved by one or more of the parties calling in an outside power, normally with disastrous results for the Omanis in general. This is the story of the First Imāmate, of the Nabahīnah, of the Yaᶜaribah and of the Al Bu Saᶜīd.[3]

Al-Wārith bin Kaᶜb al-Kharūsi became Imām, in 801 AD/ 185 AH. He is one of the early a'imma who ruled with great justice and impartiality, and was merciful to his enemies:

> He restored the good of former times among the Mussulmans, was upright in his administration, encouraging those who adhered to the truth and restraining impiety and crime, extortion and discord...[4]

The story is told by Salīl bin Razik: Al-Wārith died as he lived. He had confined a number of men in a prison, which was caught in the middle of a flash-flood. He ordered them to be freed, but no-one would risk the flood, so he attempted to cross the torrent himself. Some followed him, but they were all swept away, as were the prisoners. But thanks to him and his successors, the Ibāḍī state remained secure.[5]

This first Imāmate came to an end effectively a hundred years after it began, with the deposing of Al-Salt bin Malik al-Kharūsī in 866 AD/ 272 AH. A new alignment of tribes meant that the old alliances (centred round the Yaḥmad tribe) broke down; those in control of the more fertile coastal strip, the Bāṭinah, needed to keep others out. The ᶜAbbāsid army was called in, and destroyed many fulūj; their empire continued to dominate coastal life.

In the eleventh century local rule was only temporarily re-established. Several a'imma were elected on and off, but having limited political power or relevance. If it can be said that any tribe came out on top, the Nabahinah were such, a branch of the Azd's. Later, a'imma were chosen from the Banī Kharūs. But the internal affairs of the 'awdīyah (wādis) of the Jabal Akhḍar were of little significance to the ᶜAbbāsids, who would not have been more than a little involved with the Bāṭinah, and there only because of the development of trade along the coast.

One inherent problem for any Imām wanting to develop his power-base, was the rule that - as Imām - he could not own property. An Imām attempting to 'get round' the rule was soon mistrusted and even if a particular incumbent was not removed from office (the Ibāḍī specifically allow for the removal of an Imām who proves unworthy of office) life was then difficult if not impossible for his successor.

Such was the case of Muḥammad bin Ismāᶜīl, who succeeded in establishing military order out of the chaos created by the collapse of the Hormuzi dynasty, around 1500 AD/ 905 AH, and before the Portuguese had established themselves as a power in the region (Hormuz becoming a main base for the Portuguese). But the question then arose of how the benefits accruing should be administered. Muḥammad bin Ismāᶜīl's solution was to enforce his own control over the forts and castles. But this meant that on his death, while his son Barakat was nominated successor and was elected Imām, two others were elected alongside him. Castles on the inland (west) of the Hajar changed hands in the ensuing chaos, with alarming frequency and with much bloodshed.[6]

In 1258 AD/ 656 AH, the Mongols captured Baghdad, ending the ᶜAbbāsid caliphate, but the impact on Oman would not have been significant. On the coast a century later, as the Crusades had wakened the interest of Europe in the East, the first Portuguese were seen, who while establishing a hold over the ports of Oman in order to protect their passing trade, would have been little interested in the interior. The influence of Ṣuḥār declined, and Qalhat 100 miles south of Muscat became for a while a main centre for local trade. Then, as trade with India and East Africa developed, the Portuguese encouraged the development of Muscat. It had good anchorage and had excellent protection from the interior because of the mountains immediately around it. With rebuilt forts, Muscat took over as principal port. To the north of the Arab world, the Ottoman - Sunnī - Empire began its expansion, but did not make headway against the Safavid -Shīᶜī - dynasty in Persia, and Oman remained un-noticed by the greater powers.

Ibn Baṭṭūṭah, the 14th Century AD / 8th Century AH traveller, describes the beliefs of the Ibāḍī during this period:

> ...We entered the capital of the country (of Oman) which is the town of Nazoua (Nizwah).. Its inhabitants are accustomed to take their meals in the courts of the mosques, each one bringing what he has provided. They eat thus altogether, and travellers are admitted to eat with them. They are strong and brave, always at war among themselves. They are of the Ibāḍite sect, and go through the Friday noonday prayers four times, after which the Imām reads verses of the Qur'ān, and gives a sermon in the qutba style in which he supplicates the favour of God upon Abū Bakr and ᶜUmar, but passes over in silence ᶜUthman and ᶜAlī. When they wished to mention ᶜAlī they refer to him as 'the man', saying 'It is said concerning the man' or 'the man said...' They implore the divine favour upon that criminal, the accursed murderer of ᶜAlī, calling him 'the pious servant of God, the suppressor of sedition.'[7]

The election of Imām Nāṣir bin Murshid in 1624 AD/ 1033 AH, of the Ya^{c}ariba tribe did not seem any different from many previous attempts to bring order out of local muddle, and of no relevance to the Portuguese, now well established even in small towns between Muscat and Ṣuḥār, such as Seeb and Barkah. A translation by British political agent E.C.Ross, of the Kashf al-Ghummah describes not only this period, but underlying character traits:

> Now the people of 'Uman are endowed with certain qualities, which it is my hope they may never lose. They are a people of soaring ambition, and of haughty spirit; they brook not the control of any Sultān, and are quick to resent affront; they yield only to irresistible force, and without ever abandoning their purpose. A man of comparatively poor spirit, judged by their standard, is on a par as regards magnanimity with an Amir of any other people. Each individual aims at having the power in his own hands or in the hands of those he loves. He desires everyone to be submissive to him, and his neighbour has the same ambition. Unfortunately none is worthy of such things, but those whom God elects, pious, chaste and blessed persons, who are not swayed by their desires, nor prone to be led away by blind passions.... There were none to be found, whether dwellers in houses or dwellers in tents, whether 'Bedu' or 'Hadhr', whether on the mountain heights or in the sandy levels, but had quaffed the draught of terror, and suffered from the general destruction which encompassed religion, property, and life, except those for whom God tempered their troubles and whom He saved from the strife by His bounteous protection. In this manner (the people of Oman) ceased not to struggle in the abyss of desolation, walking in evil ways, until God vouchsafed to them the appearance of his wise servant, the Imām of the Musalmans, Nāṣir-bin Murshid-bin Malik..... [8]

Nāṣir bin Murshid did indeed prove to be a stronger Imām than his predecessors, and within 25 years a dynasty had been established, which as well as removing foreign Arabs from the interior, also saw off the Portuguese from the Omani and east African coasts. The Ibāḍī Imamate had another opportunity to prove itself. Credit must be given to Imām Nāṣir's sponsor, one of the Rustāqi ^{c}ulamā': Khamis bin Sa^{c}id al-Shaqsī. He was the author of a major Ibāḍī revivalist work: Al-Minhāj al-Ṭālibīn which details the whole body of Ibāḍī law as well as restating its ideology. He persuaded the electors to unite behind a 20 year old youth, from a clan which had little (known) history but was commanding the Rustāq area.

By the time Nāṣir bin Murshid's cousin, Sultān bin Saif (the First) succeeded him, it appeared at first that they had overcome the temptation to personal aggrandisement from their office: as well as having reasonable family fortune from their Rustāq base, they were operating through agents. In the Interior, Nāṣir had succeeded in playing off one tribe with another, and established control on both sides of the Hajar. He then turned his attention to the ports, by now controlled by the Portuguese, who had been building up their defences there. He appointed as his main General his cousin Sultān bin Saif, who succeeded in removing the Portuguese garrisons one by one. Muscat came under siege several times before Nāṣir died (April 1649 AD/ Rabiᶜ I, 1059 AH); the same day as Nāṣir's death, Sultān bin Saif was elected Imām. Assaults continued against Muscat, success coming six months later. The Portuguse returned in 1652 AD/ 1062 AH with a large naval force, and again a year later, but 'their key bases on the Oman coast went by default for reasons of cowardice and pride.' [9] The period that followed to the establishment of the Al Bu Saᶜīd dynasty in 1719 AD/ 1131 AH, is an exciting one, with campaigns and intrigues, reaching down the coast of East Africa; but, as power developed, the growing inability of the Yaᶜribi a'imma to show the necessary piety and 'other-worldliness' that should characterise an Ibāḍī Imām, created great tensions.

As funds came in from trading levies (some apparently excessive, but as it was foreigners forced to use Muscat who were charged, nobody from Oman seemed to object) so projects such as the building of the great round fort at Nizwah -replacing an older one - could be undertaken. Rules about the development of land that had fallen into disuse were changed to the favour of the developer, and Balᶜarab, one of Sultān bin Saif's sons, made the area around Jabrīn and Bahlā forts productive again. His brother, Saif bin Sultān II (who seized power from him a few years after their father's death in 1679 AD, and was formally recognised as Imām after Balᶜarab died 1692-3 AD/ 1104 AH, was given the title Master of the Land, Qayd al-Arḍ. However, the title did not mean that this growing power was universally acclaimed. Although the form of election for Imām during this period has been a well-kept secret, dissatisfaction - although not universal - was clearly growing about the kind of candidate available, not only the expected 'rubber-stamping' of the next dynastic nomination, but more particularly the swing away from the religious to the temporal. The fourth Imām personally owned 24 large ships, 28 barques and 1,700 slaves being clear evidence of the extent to which his attitude diverged from the asceticism advocated by the purist ᶜulamā'. [10]

The expansion of trade with East Africa by the Yaᶜribi a'imma, had a religious and cultural, as well as a commercial significance, which lasted up to at least 1970 AD/ 1390 AH, when the latest contingent of exiles was welcomed back to Oman, with the deposition of Sultān Saᶜid bin Taimur, by his son, Qaboos. Zanzibar, 30 miles from Dar Es Salaam, still has a sizable community with many family ties to Oman, and where the dress is still dish-dash and embroidered caps, as in Oman. Half of the 3,000 stone buildings of the old town are crumbling. After a revolution in 1964 against the Island's Sultāns, a Union was signed with newly independent Tanganyika. But many of its population want to be independent of Tanzania; a referendum has become a major political issue.

The links between East Africa and Oman began thousands of years ago, with the help of the monsoon pattern of the Indian Ocean. Every December to February, with remarkable steadiness the north-east monsoon carried craft from Oman south down the African coast; from April to September, the south-westerly monsoon carried them back.[11] The Roman author Pliny (23-79 AD) is recorded as telling in his *Natural History:*

> how the planks of Arab ships were sewn together, as many of the small boats in Oman still are, and they made use of the north-east monsoon for trading with India... Trajan mounted an expedition in 116 AD through Iraq to suppress the pirates, but did not reach as far as Oman...[12]

I found near the ruins of a frankincense port in Dhofar - Khor Rori - established originally by the Sumerians, and certainly active in Roman times - remains of ancient fortifications on what appeared to be an identical design to sections of Hadrian's Wall of Northern England. Perhaps Roman engineers reached this outpost of Empire? The reference in Pliny, to the sewn boats as a design feature was certainly continued to this century, as hulks with stitched planking can still be found rotting on Oman's beaches. Tim Severin, having previously recreated the monk Brendan's voyage across the Atlantic in a leather boat, recreated in 1976-7 AD/ 1396-7 AH, the journey of an Omani boom - design circa. 1000 AD/ 4th Century AH, from Oman to China; the vessel was built at Ṣūr, Oman, with timbers stitched together with coconut fibre.[13]

In the years before Islām, Nestorian Christians used the winds to carry them to India and beyond, even as far as Malaya.[14] But it was the same winds, that carried the first Ibāḍī exiles from Oman to East Africa, at the beginning of the first 'dark age' at the hands of the Umayyads in the closing decade of the first century of Islām. A sympathetic account of those times has recently been written in Zanzibar, by a family member of the recent exile:

> The visitors who came to these regions between the 8th and 10th centuries came here for permanent settlement, because they found no peace and safety in their homeland due to Islāmic feudal wars and religious persecutions which reigned supreme in Arabia during that period... These were the first Muslim missionaries to come down to these regions. That they preferred to leave their nativeland and

> sacrifice the material wealth in order to find a place where they could practise and preach their religious ideologies, explains clearly the extent of their religious fervour. And indeed in these regions they found a wide field for missionary work... [15]

Trade between Oman and Africa developed with the autonomy allowed by the ᶜAbbāsids; interchange of ideas continued as well alongside a developing trade, during the first Imāmate. As Oman fell back into inter-tribal wars, no doubt trade lessened, but the ties remained to develop again under the Yaᶜribi a'imma:

> The Seventeenth century is another memorable date in the annals of East Africa, in that Omani Arabs came in response to an appeal made by the ill-governed mass for military aid in their struggle against the oppressive rule of the Portuguese. With their might, they attacked and drove them away and subsequently the coast became part of the kingdom of the Imām of Muscat and Oman.[16]

With the Portuguese removed from the shores of Oman, sea battles continued for another century along the coast of East Africa. But in the body politic of Oman, civil war was festering. Not only inspired by the ᶜulamā', more immediately fuelled by an outbreak of inter-tribal warfare between the Ghāfiri and Hināwi tribes, but finally 'allowed' simply by the Yaᶜaribi family failing to get on with each other; smaller skirmishes broke into full civil war for twenty-five years.[17] In 1741 AD/ 1154 AH, with support from both Ghāfiri and Hināwi, Aḥmed bin Saᶜīd was elected Imām, following several 'preternatural events' as recorded by Percy Badger, a nineteenth century clergyman who made Arabia his particular study.[18]

The first of the Al Bu Saᶜīd dynasty was Imām for 34 years, but his strength and resources came from the sea rather than the land. Perhaps because of the debilitating effects of the civil war, there was little apparent opposition. His second son Saᶜīd succeeded him in 1783 AD/ 1197 AH, but within three years his own son Ḥāmad had raised most of the country against him. Ḥāmad's rejection of any religious sanction for his rule was made clear enough, when he left his father as Imām in Rustāq, and established his own secular court at Muscat.[19] The process had reached the apparent conclusion, again, that the dream of theocracy - epitomised by an Imām without property - was unattainable. Percy Badger said of the title of Sayyid with which Ḥāmad ruled, and his uncle Sultān bin Aḥmad who succeeded him in 1792 AD/ 1206 AH:

> ... the title so applied was an innovation; it tended moreover, to distinguish the ruling family, and to give them a corporate dignity over all the other native chiefs and grandees. The 'House of the Seyyids' like the reigning 'Houses' of Europe, has become a recognised dynasty, having the first claim to the succession.[20]

Badr bin Saif, nephew of Sultān bin Aḥmad succeeded him in 1804, but was murdered two years later by Sultān's son, Saᶜīd who - ruling for 50 years - became the greatest of the Al Bu Saᶜīd princes. But he never bothered about the title and duties of Imām. It was probable that Sayyid Saᶜīd bin Sultān simply did not see the point of maintaining the court of the Imām in the interior, away from the trading centre of Muscat; later in his reign, he was to prefer Zanzibar as a place to live.[21] Percy Badger speculates that had he wanted the title Imām, the tribes would not have accepted him. Either way, Imām Saᶜīd bin Aḥmad lived on peacefully in Rustāq until he died by 1821 AD/ 1236 AH, and no attempt being made to take his title from him; by which time it was as if no one had thought about a successor as Imām.

A more pressing problem had come to occupy the tribes of the interior - the Wahhābī incursions from central Arabia, who in their zeal for proselytising, were a clear challenge for the Ibāḍiyyah. In the circumstances, the election of a new Imām would probably have inflamed the Wahhābī, and so for nearly 50 years, a state of kitmān was again to exist.

Sayyid Saᶜīd left his subjects to fight their own interior battles, to the point where they finally rallied round the one tribe that seemed to be able to withstand the Wahhābis, the Yal Saᶜad, an Ibāḍī tribe who lived between the Hajar mountains and Ṣuḥār. Led by Ḥamūd bin 'Azzan, semi-independent governor of Ṣuḥār (Sayyid Saᶜīd had effectively given him autonomy in 1849 AD/ 1265 AH) and by his son Saif, a confederacy of northern tribes took on the task of evicting the Wahhābis, from the Bureimi oasis, which they succeeded in doing, (although it was towards the end of the 1950's AD/ 1370'S AH, before this particular dispute was settled.) But there was no love lost between father and son, and Ḥamūd had his son Saif murdered in 1850; this may have been with the encouragement of the Ibāḍī zealots, as Saif having expelled his father from Ṣuḥār, had concluded a trading agreement with the British Resident of the Gulf. Ḥamūd did not long outlive his son though - he was imprisoned by one of the sons of Sayyid Saᶜīd, Thuwaini bin Saᶜīd, who was regent in Muscat for his father; Ḥamūd was tortured to death in Muscat's infamous Fort Jalāli.[22]

Meanwhile the Muṭawiᶜah - the more devout among the Ibāḍiyyah - worked more openly for the election of a new Imām. An initial attempt at alliance with the Wahhābī Amir of Riyāḍ, Faiṣal bin Turkī al Saᶜūd failed, when a new attack on Bureimi was bought off by Thuwaini (1853 AD/ 1270 AH); three years later Sayyid Saᶜīd died, leaving his empire divided between Thuwaini in Oman, and another son Mājid in Zanzibar. The alliance was again attempted, this time focusing on fighting the Muscat agreement to join in the British desire to curb the slave trade. Choosing intrigue rather than open attack, the outcome was the patricide of Thuwaini by his son Sālim, but then the Ibāḍiyyah turned on Sālim as a Wahhābī ally. The British agent in the Gulf Col. Lewis Pelly helped him survive one attempt at his removal by an uncle, Turkī bin Saᶜīd, (who was packed off to Bombay), but in 1868 Muscat was invaded by an alliance of Ibāḍī tribesmen, and ᶜAzzan bin Qais was elected Imām in Muscat.[23]

His chief minister was Saᶜīd bin Khalfan al-Khalīlī, who may have wanted to be Imām himself, but bowed to the greater electoral influence of ᶜAzzan. But neither could influence sufficiently positively the strange alliance that had brought them to power. Neither did they attempt to hold together their two main tribal 'backers' - the Hināwi and the Ghāfiri. They were misunderstood by the British as being similar in outlook to the Wahhābī, and Percy Badger was critical of British understanding of the situation:

> It is remarkable, and by no means creditable to the British Government in India, that notwithstanding our intimate political and commercial relations with 'Oman for the last century, we know actually less of that country, beyond the coast, than we do of the Lake districts of Central Africa.[24]

But by the time his views were published, ᶜAzzan was dead.[25] Soon - with Wahhābī connivance - Turkī bin Saᶜīd having escaped his loose imprisonment in Bombay, in 1871 AD/ 1288 AH, led another attack on Muscat (also with the help of the Banī Ghāfiri). Imām 'Azzan was killed in the fighting, Saᶜīd al-Khalīlī was persuaded to surrender by Pelly, but as soon as Pelly left Muscat, was buried alive with his son, by Turkī:

> The new Sultān Turkī bin Saᶜīd put Saᶜīd bin Khalfan al-Khalīlī and his son to death by burying them alive, and announcing to the British political agent at Muscat that they had died of diarrhoea and fright....[26]

The Imāmate had lasted three years.

Attempts continued to be made by the interior tribes to overthrow the Sultān in Muscat. Turkī, in order to pay his mercenary forces raised the tax on all goods from the interior from 2 per cent to 5 per cent in 1881 AD/ 1298 AH. In 1883 AD/ 1300 AH Sāliḥ bin ᶜAlī led some tribesmen into Muscat from the mountains behind, but a British warship in the harbour saved Turkī. In 1895 AD/1302, a more serious attack was made on the town (Faiṣal bin Turkī had succeeded his father as sultān), this time 120 were killed and 140 wounded before the British persuaded the veteran Sāliḥ to withdraw. Had he succeeded, there is no clear picture as to who could have been elected Imām.[27] It was 1913 AD/ 1332 AH before a serious new attempt was made, on the death of Sultān Faiṣal.

Notes and references:

1. WILKINSON, J. C.,1972, 'Origins of the Omani state' in The Arabian Peninsular Society and Politics. Edited by D. Hopwood, London, George Allen and Unwin Ltd, p.77
2. The suggestion of Persian origin for these carved steps comes from MILES, S. B., in an article 'Across the Green Mountains', Geographical Journal 1901.
3. ibid. p.78
4. RAZIK, Salīl bin, 1871, History of the Imāms and Seyyids of Oman, translated and edited by G. P. Badger, London, (new impression Darf publishers, London 1986) p. 10
5. ibid. p. 12
6. WILKINSON, J. C., 1987, Imāmate tradition of Oman, Cambridge University Press, 1987, p.216
7. MW, 1933 No. 3,(Vol. 12) p. 280, article by SMITH, Percy, 'The Ibādhites,' quoting from the Edition of the Societe Asiatique, Vol. 11, p. 227
8. SIRHAN, Sirhan bin Sa^{c}īd bin, 1874, Annals of Oman, Book VI, translated by E. C. Ross, Calcutta, (new impression 1984, Oleander Press, Cambridge p.45
9. BATHURST, R. D., 1972, 'Maritime trade and Imamate government: two principal themes in the history of Oman to 1728' in The Arabian Peninsular Society and Politics. Edited by D. Hopgood, London, George Allen and Unwin Ltd, p99
10. ibid. p.103
11. HAWLEY, Donald, 1989, Oman and its Renaissance, Stacey International, London (revised edition) p.78
12. ibid. p. 16
13. SEVERIN, Tim, 1982, The Sinbad voyage, Hutchinson, London
14. HAWLEY, Donald, Oman and its Renaissance, op. cit. p. 182
15. FARSI, Shāban Sāleḥ, 1980, Zanzibar, Historical Accounts, Islāmic Publications, Lahore, pp. 10-11
16. ibid. p.12
17. KELLY, J. B., 1972, 'A Prevalence of Furies: Tribes, Politics and Religion in Oman and Trucial Oman' in The Arabian Peninsular, Society and Politics. Edited by D. Hopwood, London, George Allen and Unwin Ltd, p.108
18. RAZIK, Salīl bin, History of the the Imāms and Seyyids of Oman translated and edited by G. P. Badger, op. cit. p. 156
19. WILKINSON, J. C., Imāmate tradition of Oman, op. cit. p.227

20. BADGER, G. P., 'On the title of Imām' appendix one; Salīl bin Razik, 1871, History of the Imāms and Seyyids of Oman, translated and edited by G. P. Badger, London, (new impression Darf publishers, London 1986) p.377
21. KELLY J. B., 'A Prevalence of Furies' op. cit. p. 110
22. ibid. p. 111
23. WILKINSON, J. C., Imāmate tradition of Oman, op. cit. p.236
24. BADGER, G. P., in his preface to Salīl bin Razik, History of the Imāms and Seyyids of Oman, op. cit. para 7
25. KELLY, J. B., 'A Prevalence of Furies' op. cit. p. 116
26. WILKINSON, J. C., Imāmate tradition of Oman, op. cit. p.237
27. KELLY, J.B., 'A Prevalence of Furies' op. cit. p.117

5: Christianity in South & East Arabia, up to 1900 AD/ 1317 AH

Bishop Thomas Valpy French, an Englishman who had spent nearly forty years as a missionary in Lahore, becoming its first Anglican bishop, arrived in Muscat in February 1891AD/ Rajab 1309AH to open a new mission field. His grave in a rocky cove near Muscat proclaims him to be the first missionary to Muscat; but Christians had certainly lived in Muscat before. The Portuguese had had their chapels in renovated forts, even a cathedral in Muscat, which by Bishop French's time, was an arms store. Perhaps some of the Christians from the pre-Islāmic church in the Yemen, reached the anchorages further up the Arabian coast to the frankincense port of Khor Rori, near modern Ṣalalah, or the precursors of Ṣūr, Qalhat and Muscat. From the Gulf came missionaries of the Church of the East, or as it became known the Nestorian Church. At least one Bishopriç was established on what is now Oman, at Ṣuḥār. Bishop Yohannan attended the Synod of Markabta in 424 AD, Bishop David attended the consecration of Mar Aba as *Catholicos* in 544 AD, and Bishops Samuel and Stephanus from Ṣuḥār were present at the councils of 576 AD and 676 AD/ 58 AH.[1] There were also Bishoprics at Qatar, at Mashmahiq, noted as an island between Bahrain and Oman - this could be Muharraq, now connected to Bahrain by causeway, taken over as Bahrain's airport. Darin, at the southern tip of Bahrain island; and perhaps Bahrain, which was probably the mainland - now modern Dahran, although this may be the same as Mashmahiq.

Christians came to Arabia from Persia, to escape from persecution. The early Persian Church claims its origins from Thaddaeus, and that he had been sent to Edessa by Thomas; both are listed in the New Testament as disciples of Jesus. One of the treasures of the Edessene church was a letter said to have been received by them from St Thomas, in India. By the middle of the second century AD, the church of Edessa possessed the four gospels in Aramaic. By the third Century AD, it had become a centre for theological training. The Christian community there was strengthened by more than one influx of refugees from persecution by Roman Emperors, particularly Diocletian. Edessa became the seat of the *Catholicos*, of what was to be labelled the Nestorian Church, as it stood against Cyril of Alexandria (Bishop, 412-444AD). The missionary zeal of the Nestorians was great, reaching from Syria to China. The Christian church in India (the so-called St Thomas church) was almost certainly an offshoot of Nestorian Christianity.[2]

Ilse Lichtenstädter speculates how so much of pre-Islāmic history was 'purged' due to the censorship of Islāmic scholars:

> The silence of Arabic poetry on religious beliefs and the lack of expressions of religious emotions in it and in other forms of pre-

Islāmic literature were taken as proof that the Arab did not possess religiosity and was living for the here and now, without meditating upon such religious questions as life after death or the existance and presence of a divine being or beings. But that lack was due to the censorship of Islāmic scholars, who, generations later, purged all expressions of pre-Islāmic beliefs from their literary written records and substituted the name Allāh for those of pre-Islāmic deities.[3]

Excavations were undertaken in the earlier 1980's, without publicity, at Jubail (north of Bahrain) of a large church/ monastery discovered in the sand. The poet Labid (b. around 552 - 560) who was converted to Islam, 'dazzled by the beauty and eloquence of the Qur'ān' [4] refers in a description of a journey to the coastlands of the Hajar region, how he was met by the beating of wooden clappers calling to worship.[5] The beating of a wooden clapper lisān al-jaras it seems was a substitute for the bell nāqūs more usually associated with the Christian call to worship.[6]

In the century before the Prophet Muḥammad, the Jews of Yemen had a brief period of dominance, (the only time when Jews had political autonomy anywhere between the fall of Jerusalem in 70 AD, and 1948 AD/ 1367 AH); it was a time when many thousands of Christian monks and nuns are said to have been killed. Among them, the story is told of the heroic martyrdom of Princess Rohaima, who before she was killed, insisted on letting down her hair as a bride of Christ.[7] There may be reference made to this persecution in the Qur'ān Sūrah 85, Burūj - the Zodiacal signs:

4 Woe to the makers
Of the pit (of fire)
Fire supplied (abundantly)
With fuel:
5 Behold! they sat
over against the (fire),
And they witnessed
(All) that they were doing
Against the Believers......
10 Those who persecute (or draw
into temptation)
The Believers, men and women,
And do not turn
in repentance, will have
the penalty of Hell....

Perhaps these verses are a reference to this persecution of the Christians of Najrān by the Jews, and their King Zu-Nuwas.[8] Then came retribution from Abyssinia; Christian armies invaded Yemen, and drove out the Jewish rulers, re-establishing the churches there. A great new cathedral was built at Ṣanᶜā', the ruins of which remained at least until the beginning of the twentieth century.[9] But shortly after its consecration it was desecrated, and vengeance was demanded of the tribes from the north.[10] 'Intoxicated with power and fired by religious fanaticism', the Christian army marched to Makkah, and an attempt was made to clear the Kaᶜbah. The invading army included soldiers mounted on elephants, but they were repulsed, as celebrated in the Qur'ān, Sūrah 105, Fīl -the Elephant. Two months later the Prophet was born, and within a generation Christianity had apparently disappeared from Arabia.[11]

Whatever influence the Coptic and Iraqi (Nestorian) churches managed to maintain in north Arabia, there seems to have been little Christian presence in the heartland of Islām - central, south and east Arabia for many centuries after the dawn of Islām. What survived would have been in small pockets, such as in Bahrain. Nearly a thousand years were to pass, before the increase of trade with Europe in the seventeenth century meant at least a superficial meeting of religious thinking, when, in 1645 Philip Wylde, a representative of the East India Company concluded a treaty with Imām Nāṣir bin Murshid at Ṣuḥār which included the right: 'That we may have licence to exercise our own religion....' There were other clauses:

> No Christian shall have licence, in any part of this
> Kingdom, besides the English to supply this port....[12]

It would appear that Wylde's religion was being used to protect his business interests as much as anything else.

There was a meeting between Islām and Christianity, with the arrival in Muscat in April 1811 AD/ 1226 AH, of Henry Martyn; although he did not stay long, from his journals the stay clearly made an impact on him, inspiring him in his work of translating the New Testament into Arabic. 'there is a promise in reserve for the sons of Joktan.'[13] As the nineteenth century progressed, traders continued to call in to ports along the Oman coast; there were Christians among them. One such was an American captain who on his annual collection of a date cargo, would leave behind him Arabic bibles and testaments.[14] Colporteurs of the British and Foreign Bible Society followed his example on their way from India to Africa, or up into the Gulf.

The British took over Aden as a base essential to their naval operations in 1880 AD/ 1297 AH, and the coast between there and India became strategically important to the British navy. Surveys were carried out, and alongside them, Major-General Felix T.Haig surveyed the whole area for the Church Missionary Society. Haig's main report was published in 1887 AD/ 1304 AH, in the Church Missionary Intelligencer; another, focusing on the Yemen, was published in the Geographical Journal.[15] A report was written subsequently about Muscat and

Oman, focusing first on the geography and a description of the tribes of Oman, based on information from the British resident Colonel Miles. He went on to say:

> The Arabs of Oman are a finer race physically, and I am inclined to think in most other respects, than those around Aden, as well as much handsomer. They have a manly and independent bearing, and a pleasant frankness and openness of manner. There is an entire absence of anything like servility or cringing. They think themselves the finest race on the face of the earth, and their manner, while perfectly polite, is the natural expression of this feeling. They are tolerant to other religions.... The people generally were evidently pleased with the novel spectacle of an englishman conversing with them on religious questions in their own language....

The General admitted his Arabic was 'of the very humblest order.' He describes Qur'ānic schools at work, while wondering how many pupils really learned to read, rather than simple recitation. Perhaps there was a little prejudice here?

> At Somail I was told that three-fourths of the boys go to school, and I was surprised at the number of schools which I saw, the masters sitting, in many cases under the shade of the date trees, with their pupils grouped around them....

He spoke of a dispensary 'under the management of an able and much respected officer of the Bombay Medical Establishment, himself a native of India', but saw great opportunity for the establishment of 'medical aid... which would often prepare the way for Gospel teaching.' He pictured Oman as being invested with additional importance as a mission field, because:

> at its western extremity it is only 200 miles distant from Riad, the capital of Nejd, which could thus be reached without going through Turkish territory. It would appear that the shortest, easiest, and safest route into central Arabia is from this quarter....

The Oman report concludes with two paragraphs specifically about the <u>Ibāḍī</u> and what Haig believed to be one area of failure in Christian dialogue:

> The Omanese belong, with few exceptions, to the sect of Ibādhis, or followers of the teaching of Abdullāh-ibn-Ibādh, who flourished in the eighth century. They differ from the other sects of Mohammedanism in holding that the Imāmate is elective and not hereditary. Apart from this question, which touches no vital doctrine, and certain views in regard to predestination and free-will, which doctrines they are said to hold in such a sense as to make God the author of evil as well as good, their religion does not differ materially from that of the more orthodox Mohammedans. Though tolerant of other religions they appeared to me to be a more religious people that the Zeidiyeh of Yemen. The daily prayers seemed to be most regularly observed and every village I

passed through has its Musjid. Their ideas of Christianity must, in the past, have been derived from the Portuguese. These Romanists are styled "polytheists" in the Arab history of Oman, and left behind them at least one monument of their mariolatry in a chapel with an inscription to the Virgin, which still exists, though now used for very different purposes, (probably a gun store, as later described by an american missionary) in one of the ruined Portuguese forts at Muscat.'

The Omanese State was at its greatest height of power in the beginning of the present century. It then included Bahrein and Katar in the north-west, and Linja and Bundar Abbas on the opposite side of the Gulf, besides Socotra, Kishim, and Zanzibar. Socotra is now a British possession. Its population, supposed to be 3,000, or 4,000 in number, was once Christian, and still preserved a corrupt form of religion evidently derived from the mariolatry of the early missionaries when the Portuguese took the island in the sixteenth century. They had altars, and worshipped an image called "Mariam." The Portuguese protected them, but when they left the island about the middle of the century, Arabs crossed over from Kishim, and put to the sword all who refused to embrace the tenets of Islām. Since then the population have been wholly Mohammedan.' [16]

Prejudice again perhaps partly explains these views, held by one who in his last years of life became increasingly frustrated by what he considered to be the romanising tendencies of the Church of England. There would seem to be some substance however, to the charge of insensitivity to what seems to be a particularly Ibāḍī concern against images of any form, (see below, Chapter 11, page 97). It was of course not the Roman Church, the object of much Victorian Protestant invective, but Cyril of Alexandria, the scourge of the Nestorians, who developed the Mother of God debate.[17] Samuel Zwemer was to later sum up General Haig's reports:

> These are even today the best condensed statement of the needs and opportunities of this long neglected Peninsula, while his account of the problems to be met and the right sort of men to meet them, will always remain invaluable until the evangelisation of Arabia is an accomplished fact.[18]

In fact, before his substantive reports, Haig had published earlier papers, one of which was read by a young Cambridge Theology graduate, Ian Keith Falconer. After an interview with Haig, he obtained the support of his own Free Church of Scotland Foreign Mission Committee, and arrived in Aden at the end of 1885 AD/ early 1303 AH, to conduct a preliminary survey, deciding upon Sheikh Othman as the best place as a base. He returned to Britain in 1886 to prepare for his final departure, and had a hectic summer - even finding the time to attempt to persuade an insurance company to insure his life in favour of his old mission work in London's East End. He was unsuccessful! He sailed for Aden again with his young wife in the autumn. He was there for General Haig's visit in 1887 AD/ 1304 AH, but within three months had been taken ill with fever, and died.[19] But the mission continued, with hospital and slave school, to be the inspiration for other Christian missions in Arabia.

The Church Missionary Society published a resolution on the subject of Christian Mission to Islam 1888 AD/ 1305 AH:

> While the difficulties in the way of missionary work in lands under Mohammedan rule may well appear to the eye of sense most formidable, this meeting firmly persuaded, that, so long as the door of access to individual Mohammedans is open, so long it is the clear and bounden duty of the Church of Christ to make use of its opportunities for delivering the Gospel message to them, in full expectation that the power of the Holy Spirit will, in God's good time, have a signal manifestation in the triumph of Christianity in those lands.'[20]

Bishop Mackey of Uganda took up the plea for a Mission in Muscat, the following year, his concern being fired by the slaves being taken from his Diocese to the slave markets of Oman and Zanzibar. He saw Muscat:

> ....in more senses than one, the key to central Africa. I do not deny that the task is difficult; and the men selected for work in Muscat must be endowed with no small measure of the Spirit of Jesus, besides possessing such linguistic ability as to be able to reach not only the ears, but the very hearts of men. We need desperately six men, the pick of the English universities... The Arabs have helped us often, and have hindered us likewise. We owe them therefore a double debt, which I can see no more effective way of paying than by at once establishing a strong mission at their very headquarters - Muscat itself.[21]

He closed his long and carefully worded plea for a mission to Muscat: 'May it soon be said, this day, is salvation come to this house, forasmuch as he also is a son of Abraham.' Accompanying the plea, in a personal letter he said:

> I enclose a few lines on a subject which has been weighing on my mind for some time. I shall not be disappointed if you consign them to the waste-paper basket, and shall be only too glad if, on a better representation on the part of others, the subject be taken up, and something definite be done for these poor Arabs, whom I respect, but who have given me much trouble in years past. The best way by

which we can turn the edge of their opposition and convert their blasphemy into blessing is to do our utmost for their salvation. [22]

Action came from Bishop Valpy French. Having resigned his Bishopric in Lahore, he set out to learn Arabic, travelling extensively across the Middle East. His active and laughter-filled life continues to be studied in Asia and Europe. Passing through the Red Sea on his way to Muscat, guided there by a strong sense that he was to be the first to answer Bishop Mackey's call, Bishop French met some young American missionaries, and encouraged them to follow him to Muscat. He arrived there in February 1891 AD/ Rajab 1308 AH. In a letter to the Church Missionary Society, just after Easter, he wrote:

> There is much outward observance of religious forms; there are crowds of mosques; rather a large proportion of educated men and women too; the latter take special interest in religious questions, and sometimes lead the opposition to the Gospel. They have large girls' schools and female teachers. There is a lepers' village nigh at hand to the town. I occupied for the second time this morning a shed they have allotted to me, well roofed over; and these poor lepers, men and women, gathered in fair numbers to listen. Chiefly however, I reach the educated men by the roadside or in a house portico, sometimes even in a mosque, which is for me a new experience. Still there is considerable shyness, occasionally bitter opposition. yet bright faces of welcome sometimes cheer me, and help me on, and I am only surprised that so much is borne with. I have made special efforts to get into the mosques, but most often this is refused. The Moolahs and Muallims seem afraid of coming to help me on in my translations, or in encountering with me more difficult passages in the best classics. This has surprised and disconcerted me rather, but I have been saved in the main from anything like depression..... [23]

His dream was to reach into the Interior of Oman, but a few days after writing this letter, he received sunstroke on his way from Muttrah to Sib, in an open boat; one story is that he had insisted on wearing his black cassock - his only protection a black umbrella. Two days later he set out into the palm-grove with some books, but was later found collapsed under a palm-tree. He returned to Muscat, but was unconscious on arrival and hardly recovered consciousness. Taken to the British Residency, he died on May 14th 1891 AD/ 3 Shawwal 1308 AH. He was buried in the little Christian cemetery in a cove behind Muscat; described as the 'seven-tongued man', one inscription on his tomb offers justification for the several other missionary graves that were to be laid near his; as Jesus said: 'Unless a grain of wheat fall into the ground and die...'

Two American missionaries, from the Reformed (Dutch) Church Theological Seminary at New Brunswick, New Jersey, James Cantine and Samuel Zwemer, arrived at Cairo at the end of 1890 AD/ mid-1308 AH. The latter had found himself on the same steamer as Bishop French, neither knowing of the other previous to their meeting. A few weeks after the Bishop died in Muscat, Cantine arrived for a brief visit; by the end of the year Peter Zwemer, brother of Samuel, arrived to 'find out the prospects for mission work there.' Learning from the experience of a Bible colporteur who had been set upon by a bazaar mob who took a dislike to his wares, a shop was rented and bibles offered for sale, but presumably without hawking them round the lanes of the sūq. Peter Zwemer wrote '... there has been no disturbance. This fact is due, I think, to strong English political influence with H.H. the Sultān.' [24] This was to be a recurrent theme in the journals of the new mission, in Kuwait and Bahrain as well, but particularly in Muscat:

> The freedom granted to Europeans on account of the peculiar relation of the Sultan's Government to that of great Britain, in an incalculable privilege in a Mohammedan country. The scriptures may be read in public. Open discussion at either of the large city gates, in the presence of a European will not be disturbed and instruction where such is desired may freely be given.[25]

Sales encouraged the visiting missionaries, who did begin colporting their bibles to the villages either side of Muscat on the coast, and a few miles inland. Visitors to the rented house of the missionaries talked freely, and there was 'an interest in learning English.' An attack of 'dingo' fever could drive them to Bombay for convalescence, but they would return and extend their journeys by using a bedden, a fast sailing dhow up to Ṣuḥār, and towns and villages on the way. Requests for a doctor were frequent, and colourful descriptions of their hospitable receptions are described in the Field Reports to the Mission Headquarters in New Jersey. At Ṣuḥār:

> I am given a room in the fort, and a number of Arabs assembled and entertained me with questions, various and divergent, demanding to know the reason for the depreciation of silver, as well as the authority of the Prophet of Nazareth above that of the prophet of Arabia..... I am determined to occupy Muscat as a station of the Arabian Mission.[26]

At the end of 1894 AD/ mid-1312 AH, Peter Zwemer reported:

> Touring in the further regions was deemed inadvisable this quarter, on account of the many petty internal strifes, whereby mountain passes were closed and roads rendered unsafe. A certain Sheikh, who is in sympathy with the rightful heir to the throne and leads a powerful retinue, was on the warpath the greater part of October and November, even at one time threatening to besiege Muscat, as he had

> done in 1881.[27] The son of Sultān Faiṣal was Tāymur, and had:
> ....suddenly gone fanatic in 1905, adopting the mutawwiᶜ habits and entering into correspondence with 'Isa (one of the possible contenders for imam at the time) but he was soon to have been dissuaded by the British from his display of bigotry.... [28]

Peter Zwemer presumably spotted this tendency earlier! A desire to open a school which evidently had the agreement of the Sultān, was thwarted by 'a few jealous Moslem teachers, by intimidating the parents.' [29]

The first 1895 report from Muscat is dominated by a description of the city after Ṣaliḥ's raid, and there is speculation:

> had the attacking party gained the day, Muscat would now be governed by a sultan from one of the most fanatical and intolerant tribes in Arabia. We are thankful therefore, that the former mild government has been restored.... [30]

By the next report, a description of a tour south down the coast to Ṣūr and places between is offered, so political concerns seem to have dwindled in the minds of the missionaries. Again, fascinating descriptions occur, of communities now absorbed into a modern Arabian oil-state:

> An allnight tack against headwinds bring us to Teewe, a double village nestling on both sides of a wadi, through which runs a stream wide enough to admit the small coastal craft. The two villages are inhabited by two different and hostile tribes. They are not more than two hundred yards apart, yet each is protected from the other by a complete wall, gates and forts. Another illustration of the truth of the prediction: 'His hand will be against every man, and every man's hand against him.' We remain here a day on our way down, freely reading and explaining the Scriptures, in their primitive bazaar and coffee shops.[31]

Only in 1989 has the stream been forded by a road. I have a piece of video-film, which shows a re-enactment of the meeting of the two tribes, with dancing and music and much brandishing of weaponry, to the delight of the children of both villages.

At Ṣūr, an active slaving centre was encountered:

> Transportation being easily effected under the tricolor, which defies British inspection. Ṣūr is the terminus of several slave routes to the interior... [32]

But the missionaries did not have to go so far from Muscat to find the slave-trade in full operation. When it was too hot to travel by road, they took the easy sea journey to Banda Jissa:

> Both on account of the heat, and the employment of an excellent language teacher, giving opportunity for further language study and translation, no time was given to extensive tours. Besides the vicinity of Muscat, Jissa, a most interesting and peculiar place, a half-day's journey south of Muscat was visited. This Jissa is a small harbour, entirely invisible from the sea, and owned by a wealthy Arab sheikh, whose family and retinue are the only inhabitants; and who, in this secluded place, with its road to the interior, avoid customs dues, and trade in slaves with a free hand.[33]

It is now a 20 minute drive on an amazing road sliced through the mountains, to reach Jissa from Muscat.

In 1896 AD/ 1314 AH, the hoped-for school was established, not with children from Muscat, but rather freed slave-boys, 'signed-for' from the British Embassy, having been rescued from a slave dhow, raided in accordance with the permission of the 'Brussels Conference.' Normally such freed slaves were taken by the British to Bombay where they would be found work. A small printing press was evidently printing tracts; at one time the Sultān intervened in requesting the American Consul to stop the distribution of one offending tract. Then, as reported in the 1896/7 Field Reports, two major tours were undertaken to the interior by camel; first to Rustāq and towns and villages on the way, Scriptures were sold as the missionaries progressed; one 'fanatical Mullah' gave orders the tracts should be returned, but only a few apparently were.

The wādī town of Samail is described, (which still has large date plantations either side of a long shallow wādī.)

> The Samail valley is perhaps the most populous district in Eastern Oman and the home of the famous Muscat date. Unhappily the valley is inhabited by two hostile tribes - the Ghāferi and the Hināwee - and there is almost continual inter-tribal war.[34]

A few years later Cantine was to describe Zikki, beyond Samail

> The queerest town I have met with, a threefold split -three distinct settlements, two are the towns, heavily walled, of the hostile tribes, and the third is the immense fort or castle held by the Sultān directly between the two and not a hundred yards from either..... I pitied the condition of the Sultān's deputy, a young man of his own family, which was virtually that of a prisoner. (Another tragedy was recalled....) by the clanking chains of a mere boy, the survivor of a massacre on the mountains, and on fleeing to the Sultān had been imprisoned for safe keeping, probably with a view to some future dealing with the murderer...[35]

The second inland 'tour' was in 1897 AD/ 1414-5 AH, and took Peter Zwemer over Jabal Akhdar to Nizwah, 'divided between Sultān and it's Sheikh, with suspicion on all sides, and frequent hostile outbreaks.' [36] In 1898 AD/ mid-1316 AH, Peter Zwemer was back in the United States, fighting off fever attacks; he seemed to recover, but then died in October. He was replaced by a new missionary, George Stone, who took over the ex-slave school, but within a few months he too was dead from fever. His grave is near that of Bishop French. Another inscription on the Bishop's grave speaks for all the missionaries buried there:

> Even as the Son of Man came not to be ministered unto but to minister, and to give His life a ransom for many.[37]

Notes and references:

1. TRIMINGHAM, J. Spencer, 1979, Christianity among the Arabs in Pre-Islāmic Times, Longman London
2. STEWART, Revd John, 1928, Nestorian Missionary Enterprise, the Story of a Church on Fire, Christian Literature Society for India, Madras, republished in 1961 by Mar Narsai Press, Trichur, Kerala, pp. 2ff, also p. 53. Beth Qatraye.is probably Qatar, it is marked as being opposite Masirah Island off the east coast of Oman, on the map in the article: 'Expansion of Christianity 600 - 1500,' Times Atlas of World History, 1986, Times Books London, p101.
3. LICHTENSTADTER, Ilse, 1976, Introduction to Classical Arabic Literature, Schocken, New York, p.16
4. ULLAH, Najib, 1963, Islāmic Literature, Washington Square Press, New York, pp. 10, 30
5. TRIMINGHAM, J. Spencer, Christianity among the Arabs in Pre-Islāmic Times, op. cit. p.282
6. LYALL, Charles James, 1930, Translations of Ancient Arab Poetry Columbia University Press, New York, pp. 92-93
7. BAILEY, Kenneth, 1989, in lecture to the Middle East Council of Churches (Gulf Churches) conference.
8. Qur'ān, p.1714 - footnote 6055
9. ZWEMER, Samuel, 1900, Arabia, the cradle of Islām, p. 313
10. ibid. p. 310
11 Qur'ān, p.1791, and p.1792 - footnotes 6270-6275
12. SKEET, Ian, 1985, Oman before 1970, the end of an era, Faber and Faber, London, p.212 (First published as Muscat and Oman,the end of an era 1974)

13. ZWEMER, Samuel, Arabia, the cradle of Islām, op. cit. p.318
14. ibid. p. 320
15. Geographical Journal, London, Vol IX, p. 479
16. HAIG, C. A., 1902, Memories of the Life of General F. T. Haig by his wife, Marshall Brothers, London, pp.178-181
17. CAMPENHAUSEN, Hans von, 1963, The Fathers of the Greek Church, A. and C. Black, London, p. 166
18. ZWEMER, Samuel, Arabia, the cradle of Islām, op. cit. p.322
19. ibid. p. 341
20. ibid. p. 374
21. ibid. p. 330
22. ibid. p. 329, quoting his sister's Mackey of Uganda,New York 1897, pp. 417ff.)
23. ibid. p. 350 (quoting letters which appeared in the Church Missionary Intelligencer, for May and July 1891.)
24. NA/AC, 1st quarter,(No9) 1894, p.7
25. ibid. 2nd and 3rd quarter, (Nos 10 and 11) 1894, p.7
26. ibid. 2nd and 3rd quarter, (Nos 10 and 11) 1894, p.10
27. ibid. 1st quarter, (No 13) 1895, p.9
28. WILKINSON, J. C., 1987, The Imāmate Tradition of Oman, Cambridge University Press, p.242 - quoting (India Office Report?) Lorimer 1915 iA, 588
29. NA/AC, 1st quarter, (No 13) 1895, p.9
30. ibid. 3rd Quarter, (No 15) 1895, p.9
31. ibid. 4th Quarter, (No 16) 1895, p.10
32. ibid. 4th Quarter, (No 16) 1895, p.10
33. ibid. 3rd Quarter, (No 19) 1896, p.9
34. ibid. 4th Quarter, (No 20) 1896, p.10
35. ibid. 3rd Quarter, 1901, p. 14. This report also recorded the death of Major-General F.T. Haig, and gives a very warm glimpse of the man who had done much to inspire the missionaries of the 1890's to Arabia.
36. ibid. 1st Quarter, 1897, p. 11
37. STACEY, Vivienne, 1982, Thomas Valpy French, Church Missionary Society, London (Christian Study Centre).

6: Sultān and Imām, 1900 - 1930 AD / 1317 - 1349 AH:

If the American missionaries were happy with the 'mild government' of Sultān Faiṣal bin Turkī, there was considerable discontent from inland Oman. One of the instigators of the 1895 AD/ 1313 AH rebellion, had been ᶜAbdullāh bin Ḥumaiyad al-Sālimī, a blind scholar whose influence grew after the rebellion led by Saliḥ bin ᶜAlī had failed. To ᶜAbdullāh al-Sālimī, Sultān Faiṣal bin Turkī was little better than a kāfir. Although an Ibāḍī himself, he had failed in applying the Sharīᶜah strictly, and evidently could not speak, read, or write literary Arabic, preferring Gujerati for conversation.[1] Tension simmered between Sultān and Ibāḍiyyah. The interpreters of the law, the ones on whom the responsibility for electing a new Imām would normally fall, and who were to be found in all of the tribal groupings,[2] called the ᶜulamā', were unable to agree among themselves as to one man around whom they could unite. A decade of tribal wars, assassinations, the taking and retaking of forts, principally Rustāq,[3] meant that the Sultān in Muscat was safe from serious attack, as long as he did not give cause for his enemies to unite against him.

Then, perhaps feeling stronger than he in fact was, Faiṣal having previously turned a blind eye to issues such as a continuing slave trade, decided that he needed to control the flow of arms into Oman, and so set up a central warehouse in Muscat for their distribution. The leaders of the coalition of Hināwi Sharqīya - Banī Ruwāha - Rustāq tribes joined forces with the Ghāfirī, and they came together at Tanuf, convened by Himyar bin Nāṣir whose home it was, and with the support of ᶜAbdullāh al-Sālimī; they elected as Imām Sālim bin Rāshid of the Banī Kharūs, in May 1913 AD/ I Jamada 1331 AH. ᶜAbdullāh al-Sālimī had been working long and hard for this moment, linking up with the growing international Ibāḍī movement, particularly leaders in North Africa, the Algeria and Tunisia.[4] Within a month they succeeded in expelling the Sultān's garrison from Nizwah. Two months later the army of the Imām reached Samail. At that point the old Sultān died, and the reign of Sultān Tāymur bin Faiṣal began, in less than auspicious circumstances.

Another milestone in Ibāḍī history was passed, with the death of 94 year old Muḥammad bin Yūsuf bin ᶜIsa bin Ṣāliḥ Aṭfiyash, in 1914 AD/ 1332 AH. He was a contemporary of ᶜAbdullāh al-Sālimī, and had maintained Ibāḍī insights in the west - in North Africa. He brought about a real renaissance in Ibāḍī studies, through his extensive literary activity (his library remains to inspire the Ibāḍī scholars of the Mzab today), which was paralleled with increasing strictness in religious practice and social life.[5] Clearly, the vigour of the Ibāḍiyyah of Oman in the following decades, owed much to the leadership of Aṭfiyash, as well as al-Sālimī who with his book Tuḥfat al-aᶜyān bi-sīrat ahl ᶜUmān contributed so much to inspire the Ibāḍī to restore a full Imāmate.[6]

The confederacy at Tanuf, as well as electing Sālim bin Rāshid al-Kharūṣī as Imām, had declared Sultān Faiṣal deposed. Sultān Tāymur therefore had to move fast to attempt to re-establish what little authority the Muscat Sultāns had been able to exercise over the interior. The British government authorised a bombardment of the forces of the Imām from the sea in April 1914 AD/ Jumad I 1332, in support of the Sultān, and despite pre-occupation with larger theatres of war, in early 1915 AD/ 1333 AH, had 700 Anglo-Indian troops dug in at Bait-al-Falaj, defending Muttrah and Muscat from attack from inland. 3,000 supporters of the Imām were driven out of the coastal Bāṭinah plain, and back into the mountains.[7] The unity of the Imāmate forces broke up, with the usual skirmishes, and forts changing hands. With the end of the World War, the British focused more attention on Oman, and encouraged the Sultān to increase customs dues on date exports from 5% to 25%, perhaps intentionally to precipitate a crisis. The crisis came from another direction however: Imām Sālim bin Rāshid was killed in July 1920 AD/ Shawwal 1338 AH, by a Wahiba tribesman.

Muḥammad bin ᶜAbdullāh al-Khalīlī was elected Imām as Sālim's successor, grandson of Saᶜīd bin Khalfān al-Khalīlī, who had been instrumental in the election of 'Azzan bin Qais as Imām 60 years previously. His first task was to settle with the heavy pressure applied by the British Agent Wingate, acting for the Sultān, and to decide whether or not to sign the proposed Treaty of Seeb, a small village on the coast opposite the gap through the mountains at Samail. Imām Muḥammad al-Khalīlī did sign, and perhaps appeared by doing so, to be aquiescing to the Sultān and his British backers. Events were to prove that he was as good a compromiser as the Sultān. The Treaty was signed in October 1920 AD/ Safar 1339 AH. Wingate himself commented that

> the phraseology of the document was deliberately ambiguous and that the intention was to lead the tribes into believing that they had their independence while at the same time the British government could deny to the Sultan that the arrangements they had made derogated from his overall sovereignty.[8]

The fact that the Treaty of Seeb did in fact hold for over thirty years, is tribute more to the personalities of Sultān and Imām, and their desire for peaceful co-existence, than to any clever wording. But perhaps Wingate can be given credit for producing a treaty that fitted not only the personality of the main protagonists, but also accepted the complicated history of their relationship. What the treaty did not do, was make it any easier for those interested in development of Oman's resources, particularly the newly established oil companies. Edward Henderson, the agent for one of these companies, described his difficulty:

> The problem in Oman was that although the Sultān, Saiyid Saᶜīd bin Taimor was the overall sovereign, a part of the interior... was under an Ibāḍī Imām. In 1921 an agreement had been signed.... whereby the senior tribal sheikhs were granted considerable freedom, and in effect, something approaching autonomy in all local affairs. The Imām was not named in this document, the Sultān did not of course wish to imply recognition of his office as Imām.. to recognise him would imply that he was the sovereign of the state, rather than the Sultān himself. This agreement represented a difficulty for our company.' [9]

In 1923 AD/ 1341 AH, Sultān Tāymur gave an undertaking to the British, in which he said, 'We will not exploit any petroleum which may be found anywhere within our territories and will not grant permission for its exploitation without consulting the Political Agent at Muscat and without the approval of the High Government of India.' Kuwait, Bahrain, Qatar, and the Trucial States have given similar assurances previously.[10] In 1925 AD/ 1344 AH, the D'Arcy Exploration Company, (later to be part of British Petroleum) obtained a two year licence from Saᶜīd Tāymur, and various exploration parties explored into the mountains of the Hajar, from the Bāṭinah. They were not able to penetrate to where oil was eventually discovered well inland from the Hajar, because the Saudis decided to send tax collectors to the Bureimi area, to which the Imām also sent an armed force, to assert Imāmate control (in the event of Sultān Tāymur's prevarication). The fact that there was stalemate for a time, was due to the Imām not having sufficient confidence from the tribes involved, as well as Saudi tentativeness.[11]

Ten years elapsed, before a consortium of western oil companies, having formed the Iraq Petroleum Company, formed the company 'Petroleum Development Oman.' It is significant that the apparently abitrary decision had been made to replace the title 'Oman' in place of the originally proposed 'Muscat'.

> The problem of defining frontiers was studiously avoided and a clause (Article 12) was taken from the 1925 D'Arcy concession to meet the political situation: 'The company recognises that certain parts of the Sultān's Territory are not at present safe for its operations. The Sultān undertakes on his part to use his good offices with a view to making it possible for representatives of the company to enter such parts and will inform the company as soon as such parts become safe.' The additional words from the 1925 document 'The decision of the Political Agent Muscat regarding the safety of any area will be final,' as too the word 'Independent' before 'Ruler' in the preamble were deleted at H.M.G.'s suggestion.[12]

As for Imām Muḥammad al-Khalīlī, his diplomatic skills were being stretched as far as those of any of his Imāmate predecessors. The ᶜulamā', and the Tamīmah (paramount sheikhs, or even Amir) of the various tribes, all had their own ideas as to how the Imām should be the Imām. The fact was, Imām Sālim bin Rashīd had not had the support of the Tamīmah of the Hināwi tribes, who saw his election as a coup by the Ghāfiri tribe; they had aquiesced, but came out on top when it came to the election of Imām Muḥammad al-Khalīlī. There was constant vigilance needed, to see that two of the main tribal groupings in the Imāmate did not start, yet again, tearing themselves apart. He was certainly politically astute, as he showed when - during Sālim's Imāmate, he had been left in command of the major fort of Samail, the family home - but chose to surrender it to the Imām, rather than precipitate a war. (His father who had entrusted him with the task of holding out, while his other brother had been sent to Muscat to obtain the Sultān's help against the Imām, never forgave Muḥammad). But his ability to steer a middle course was firmly established.

The Hināwi, Ghāfiri, and all the other tribes of the Interior, would not have condoned the Sultān's flirting with the British politically, and the American missionaries coming in under their wing. Sultān Faiṣal bin Turkī, was clearly beyond redemption, and his son, despite flirting with the Muṭawwiᶜ (an extreme sect of the Ibāḍī), and despite being officially at peace with the Imām - via the Treaty of Seeb, was still very suspect. But, Imām Muḥammad al-Khalīlī did eventually meet the missionaries, and came to appreciate their presence, along with many others in the Jabal Akhḍar.

NOTES AND REFERENCES:

1. KELLY, J. B.,1972, 'A Prevalence of Furies: Tribes, Politics and Religion in Oman and Trucial Oman' in The Arabian Peninsula, Society and Politics. Edited by D. Hopgood, London, George Allen and Unwin Ltd, p.118
2. WILKINSON, J. C., 1987, The Imāmate tradition of Oman, Cambridge University Press, p.187-9. There is a detailed definition of the role of the ᶜulamā'. Also on pp. 179 of the role of qāḍī (judge appointed officially) and of a wālī (governor of a city, town or village).
3. ibid. p.241
4. ibid. p.244
5. EI², Vol. I, p. 736.
6. ᶜUBAYDLĪ, Aḥmad, Early Islāmic Oman and early Ibāḍism in the Arabic Sources, Cambridge Ph. D. Thesis, p. 5

7. Dramatic accounts of this battle, with mural paintings, retell the story to visitors to the Sultān's military museum, opened in the old fort at Beit-al-Falaj, Muscat, in 1989.
8. SKEET, Ian, 1985, Oman before 1970, the end of an era Faber and Faber, London, p.99
9. HENDERSON,Edward, 1988, This strange eventful history, Quartet books, London, p.41
10. WILKINSON, J. C., The Imāmate tradition of Oman, op. cit., p.274
11. ibid. p.259
12. ibid. p,276 In a footnote, Wilkinson says: A report of the U.S. Department of State of February 1938 (Porter 1982, 57-68) also notes: 'The present Sultān is somewhat sensitive in the matter of British control and is inclined to become increasingly assertive on the point.'

7: Christians in Oman 1900 - 1930 AD / 1317 - 1349 AH.

1901 AD/ 1317 AH saw Muscat connected to a telegraphic cable between Europe and India. Although a sovereign state, this inevitably gave the British Agency greater influence, as the India Office could so easily give advice and where necessary, prompt military support when needed. Lord Curzon visited Muscat in 1903 as Viceroy of India.[1]

The death of the first nineteenth century missionaries to Oman did not deter others. James Cantine came down from the Gulf at the end of 1899 AD, mid-1317 AH, to man the station, and after some months with the school managed to tour up the coast north of Muscat. Later in 1900 AD/ 1318 AH, Samuel Zwemer, entered Oman from the east, using a pass north of Bureimi, (skirting the main dissaffected tribal areas) and then by camel and boat made it to Muscat in time to spend half an hour with Cantine before leaving on a mail steamship to return to Bahrain. In the same journal recording that trip, Cantine described a visit to the brother of the Sultān in Muscat:

> There is the usual oriental jealousy and fear between the Sultān and his brother - it is said they never see each other except in the presence of their followers, all armed... He had in a prominent place in his reception room a copy of the Bible and New Testament, he evidently wished to impress me with his open-mindedness, but from his conversation, it was evident that his acquaintance with the book was very slight...[2]

Another missionary arrived in the summer of 1900 AD/ early 1318 AH, Harry Wiersum. He managed an interior visit with Cantine, to towns and villages around the edge of the Jabal Akhḍar, but because of news of tribal battles, they were advised not to press too far into the wādī. 'God willing, the visit to Gebel Akhḍor and the region beyond is still in store for me' he wrote in his first, and what turned out to be his last report, as he too was soon a victim of fever, which took his life while he was at Basrah.[3]

Samuel Zwemer, brother of Peter who had died in 1898 AD/ 1316 AH, was beginning to enquire about the different sects of Islām that his mission was encountering around the Gulf. Initial descriptions were later revised, particularly with regard to the Ibāḍī. He made another trip across from the east, this time staying at Bureimi, with its seven villages, and 'the people nearly all Wahhābi moslems, although they do not observe all the strictness of their sect.' Passing into Oman and up into the mountains, he observed:

The tribes here perpetually feud with each other. Everyone gets up armed and goes to bed with a rifle by his side. The people cultivate the soil and raise all sorts of small crops by careful irrigation. They belong mostly to the Abādhi sect; one of the heretical Moslem sects that grew on the soil of Persian speculation, and is less rigid in its orthodoxy and more lax in its practice than the Wahhābis...[4]

By 1911 however, Samuel Zwemer was writing much more sympathetically about the Ibāḍī, as in the National Geographic Magazine. Alongside a positive article, was a photograph of Sultān Faiṣal bin Turkī resplendent in his regalia, and a description of him as a progressive ruler with the closest relations with the government of India. The article concludes with an enigmatic and tantalisingly brief description of the Arabs of Oman as:

> ...remarkably free from fanaticism, simple in their habits, and wonderful in their hospitality. Most of them belong to the Abādhi sect, which has many beliefs in common with Christianity, and the experience of our missionaries has been that the people are not only accessible, but willing to learn, and many of them eager not only for medical help, but for teaching.[5]

The rest of Zwemer's long life was dedicated to furthering his understanding of the mind and theology of Muslims,

> Some scholars consider his first hand observations and discerning accounts of popular Islam his most exacting contribution to scholarship. Undoubtably he was one of the better informed Westerners of his day regarding contemporary Muslim belief and practice. His 'Factual Surveys' and statistics on the Muslim World within each decade fall into this group, and which he shared with others through his editorship of The Muslim World.[6]

Contacts with the Ibāḍī heartland became much more difficult during the first two decades of the twentieth century. The interior travels of the missionaries were to be severely curtailed, as the simmering of the mountain tribes reached again boiling point. Another attempt at re-establishing the Imāmate was made, this time successfully.

During this period, the American Mission had been quietly continuing its medical work in Muscat and nearby Muttrah, and its school in Muscat for freed slaveboys; four sons of Sayyid Muḥammad, brother of Sultān Faiṣal bin Turkī, attended the school.[7] A great deal of energy was expended on the necessary buildings for their work. Old buildings that had been purchased needed replacing, in the incredible heat of Muscat's bowl of mountains:

> operations were carried on only when the missionary was at hand to direct, and whenever other claims, such as mission meetings, touring, vacations etc., took precedence, then the work had to stop, as it was found that the native workmen could not be depended upon, not even for one day. When other buildings of foreign design have been put up in Muscat an architect and contractor have been obtained from India, but this was entirely beyond our means. However, having seen nearly every stone put in its place, we knew just what we had, and were assured beyond doubt of the permanence of our work.

The fact the building still remains in use by the Mission speaks well for James Cantine, the resident missionary. Unlike a neighbour's building being erected at the time:

> ...parts of which fell down several times while it was being put up. The new mission building had three foot thick walls, made of hard, brittle rock broken off the neighbouring mountainside, laid up in a mortar composed of mud, with a little sprinkling of lime... A half dozen iron beams, which excited the admiration and wonder of the natives from the interior, were, I presume, from England.[8]

The workforce comprised several nationalities: 'Arabs, Persians Balooches and Negroes', and their wages were 'between four and thirty cents a day.'

> They also insisted that the blood of a sacrifice (of course an edible one) must be shed in the foundation trenches before work was begun.[9]

In Muttrah, Dr Sharon Thoms arrived in 1909, as recalled 35 years later by another Mission doctor C. S. G. Mylrea, who spent a lifetime's service in Bahrain and Kuwait, but visited Oman several times. Dr Sharon Thoms came with his family:

> ...to lay the foundation of medical work in Oman. They were living in a funny little house on the beach. I can still see, with the eye of memory, little Wells Thoms and his sisters leaning far out over the verandah to watch their father operating in the courtyard below..... Sharon Thoms was an ideal man for those pioneer days and his friendships, accumulated in the course of his travels through the country round, endure to this day, while in the towns of Muscat and Muttrah he was universally beloved. His death in January 1913 was a heavy blow to our work.[10]

Others came to share the work, both at the hospitals and school - Revd Fred Barny, Dr Harrison, Mr and Mrs Dykstra. 'Touring' as they called it, was clearly a pleasant, if rather strenuous, diversion from the pressures and heat of Muscat and Muttrah. As Dr Mylrea observed:

> One of the things which impresses the visitor to Oman is the extraordinary friendliness of the people. Most travellers to Oman have stressed this point, and to me, coming from the dour Wahhābi north, the reception we received everywhere was delightful.[11]

His welcome was to be repeated, both to missionaries, and to expatriate workers.

Notes and references:

1. HAWLEY, Donald, 1977, Oman and its Renaissance, Stacey International, London, p.48
2. NA/AC, 1900, 2nd Quarter, p.9
3. ibid. 3rd Quarter, 1900, p.11
4. ibid. 2nd Quarter, 1901, p.12
5. National Geographic, January 1911, pp. 89-98
6. WERFF, Lyle L.Vander, 1977, Christian Mission to Muslims - the Record, William Carey Library, 533 Hermosa St., South Pasadena 91030, USA, p. 232. Samuel Zwemer was editor from 1911-1938 of The Moslem World (Muslim World after 1947), Vols. I-VI published by Christian Literature Society for India, London. Vols. VII-XXVII by Missionary Review Pub. Co., New York, Vols. XXVIII-present by Hartford Seminary Foundation, Hartford, Conn. USA.
7. CANTINE, James, and ZWEMER, Samuel M., 1938, The Golden Milestone, Fleming H. Revell Co., London, p.100
8. ibid. pp.130-1
9. ibid. p.132
10. NA/AC, 1943, first half year, p.4
11. ibid p.6.

8: Sultān, Imām, and Christian in Oman since 1930 AD/ 1349 AH

Travelling had continued to be a priority with the American missionaries, but inevitably, having to be fitted in with the pressures of running hospitals and a school, in a climate where half the year temperatures would regularly reach 40 degrees centigrade. Their reports in the Quarterly Journal of the Mission consistently reveal the friendliness and welcome they received, but as seen in C.S.G.Mylrea's comment, noted at the end of the last chapter, Ibāḍī Islām was not always given credit. I think from the tone of the articles, it was simply that the question does not seem to be a significant one to them: 'Is this something to do inherently with what the Ibāḍī believe?' Samuel Zwemer had of course implied this, in his National Geographic, 1911 article, but it seems generally sufficient, that the people the missionaries were trying to serve, were simply friendly Muslims.

Travelling missionaries did however, keep the courtesy of always calling first on the Wālī or headman of the villages they visited. Tamīmah and ᶜulamā' would have been among those on whom they called, and to whom they were often able to offer medical assistance. This did lead them to direct contact with the Imām, in the person of Dr Wells Thoms, son of Dr. Sharon Thoms. There are detailed accounts of his first meeting with Imām Muḥammad al-Khalīlī at the end of 1940 AD/ 1359 AH; the first account appeared in the Mission Quarterly News, January 1941:

> I have been over the Jebel Akhḍar (the "Green Mountains" of Arabia) and into Oman beyond. For years I have dreamed about the mountains, hoping to see them one day. Just the name held enchantment and beckoned one to search them out. On the 26th November (1940) came my chance. Into the midst of my busy Monday clinic intruded a white-turbaned soldier of the Imām of Oman bearing a letter from Sheikh Sulaiman bin Himyar of the mountain region urging me to come with all haste to treat one of his subjects who had been gored by a bull... [1]

Dr Wells Thoms was able to drive from Muscat to Rustāq, which was only fifty kilometres from Nizwah, but across the Hajar. After several days journey, which included open-air clinics with people who had never before met a westerner, and a strenuous ascent up one of the zig-zagging, almost vertical paths on the face of Jabal Akhḍar, the Doctor and his travelling companions reached Tanuf, only to discover their patient was one more day's journey away. The patient had survived, despite the accident being twenty-three days before and despite a fever and severe pain; he soon responded to the Doctor's ministrations. The Doctor then had to visit Sheikh Suleiman, and treat people in his village, being (as he thought) the second Doctor to call there, as a colleague had visited four years previously. But it then turned out in conversation with the wife of his guide, that she had been treated by Sharon Thoms 28 years previously 'When I told her that he was my father, she wept for joy... she said they had never known a man like him.' [2] On the 7th December, Nizwah was reached. There, Wells Thoms was invited to meet the Imām; his account in the report he wrote immediately, simply records the fact that, 'we treated patients on arriving, visited the Imām in his courtroom inside of a huge round tower which forms the central part of his citadel, and left Nizwah about sunset...' A fuller account of the meeting was later written, and is worth recording in full:

> We were led past crowds of people standing outside the fort, through a large outer gate and a smaller inner gate and then up two flights of stairs to the majlis or audience chamber of the Imām. When our eyes became adjusted to the dim light of the interior, we saw a thin old man wearing a large white turban on his head and sitting on a rug at the further end of a rather long room. On his right were a couple of other old men similarly attired and on either side of him were seated his bodyguard of armed men. When we entered he arose to shake our hands and then his frailness was even more apparent, for he seemed to sway a bit when he was in the upright position and his hand-clasp was not strong. He indicated with his hand that he wanted me to sit next to him but when I protested and said that Mr Dykstra was my elder and also my spiritual adviser he asked Mr Dykstra to sit on his right and me on his left. The coffee and halwah were next passed and then the rose water was sprinkled over us. While this was going on he asked us numerous questions about our purpose in leaving our country to live and work in Muscat. When we answered him that Jesus, the Anointed one, whose followers we were, ordered his followers to go to all nations to teach men His doctrines, heal the sick and share with all men the good news of the Injil (the Arabic word for the Gospel), he said, 'Do you believe that God is One?' When we said 'yes' he said, 'You are not an idolater or kāfir, you are 'the people of the book.' We believe you are mistaken in some of your doctrines but we respect you because you fear God, the Praised and Exalted One; therefore you may proceed in safety in our land. May God give you skill and wisdom to heal the sick man. I will send another guide to take you to your patient...' This began a long and happy acquaintance with this most unusual Muslim spiritual leader. He lived very simply. He and his one wife and daughter lived in two or three rooms in part of the great round tower fort of Nizwah. His only visible possessions were a few worn rugs, two score books, a few mattresses, pillows and blankets, a rifle, a dagger and a few changes of raiment. He was

known to be a just and strict disciplinarian. Murderers and thieves were usually tracked down and punished - the former were turned over to the relatives of the murdered person to be dealt with, the means of retribution being modelled in the fashion of the murder. Theft was usually punished by imprisonment. On more than one occasion I saw prisoners, bearing shackles around the ankles to each of which was fastened, by means of three-foot long chains, heavy iron balls, sitting with the soldiers at the entrance of the fort, drinking coffee and conversing quite cheerfully. He was kind and sympathetic to the poor, orphans and widows. During his lifetime most of the income from sale of dates from palm gardens belonging to the awqāf, or department of religious endowments, was given to the poor and needy. He himself was incorruptible and remained a poor man until the day of his death.[3]

The influence of the hospitals at Muscat and Muttrah were felt across the jointly-ruled territories of Sultān and Imām, as people would undertook many days journey in order to receive medical attention from the mission hospitals. By the 1940's several of the staff were from India. Many conversations and written tributes, also in novel form[4] as well as in the Mission Journal, many stories are told of long treks to receive cures from the Mission hospital. Dr. Wells Thoms reports in the 1943 Mission Journal:

Dr Job, my able Indian assistant, put in a full year of steady work, including two tours... While I was away on tours, he was in charge of the hospital, conducting the regular morning services for the staff and patients.... Nurse Mary, also from India, carried on the clinics at the Muscat dispensary for women. She had a busy year, and with excellent health was able to keep the dispensary open every weekday in the year.

In the same article by Dr Thoms, headed, 'A remarkable dream':

An Arab qāḍi (judge) who was being treated for a huge leg ulcer had a remarkable dream which considerably affected his life. The ulcer had baffled us for quite a long time. It was surrounded by an area of eczema which seemed to get worse no matter what we did for it. One evening I decided to try painting the edematous area with a triple dye solution and applying a paste of sulphonamide and zinc oxide mixed with shark liver oil to the ulcer area The next morning when I came to treat his ulcer with this combination of drugs he told me that he had had a vision that night. He said: 'Last night I was worried about my leg. I was afraid that it would not heal, and I could not sleep well because of the burning and itching. Then I saw a person in shining clothes come to me and tell me not to worry. He said that the doctor would bring some dark lotion and white ointment and apply them to my leg and that it would heal. He spoke to me so kindly that I knew it must be Jesus the Christ who spoke to me. He left me and I felt sure that I would get well, so I fell into a deep and restful sleep. I am sure that this medicine that you have brought will heal my leg.' The remarkable thing is that the leg healed completely in a very short time. Before he left the hospital he read all of the four Gospels and the Acts of the Apostles, and took them with him, back to his home in the mountains. The man's enthusiasm was an inspiration to us all.[5]

When Sultān Tāymur bin Faiṣal abdicated in favour of his son Saᶜīd, in 1932 AD/ 1350 AH, there had been no great change in relations with the Imāmate, each side apparently finding it easier to live peaceably than at war. Similarly, within the territory of Imām Muḥammad al-Khalīlī, his rule was considerably dispersed: Sheikh Sulaiman bin Ḥamyar was clearly 'de facto' in control on the high Hajar. On at least two occasions, he encouraged Dr Thoms to consider establishing a hospital on the mountain. The first time, offering by letter a house; the second time promising to build a road and to provide a truck, and to ask the Imām for land on which to build a Hospital.[6] The Sheikh called on Dr Thoms, when in Muscat to hold together the uneasy alliance between mountain and coast.

The Sultān continued to value the presence of the medical staff, inviting the Thoms family twice to Ṣalalah, flying them there and back, and receiving valuable advice on how to keep the Dhofar wells free from mosquitoes by stocking them with fish.[7] Both Sultān and Imām could hardly have been under any illusions as to the preaching work of the missionaries, and could not have been ignorant of the slowly growing congregation in Muscat, which included indigenous Omanis, and which necessitated church extensions, regularly reported in the Mission Quarterly Reports, to encourage support from home.[8] The Sultān was happy to open the new Muttrah hospital unveiling a plaque commemorating the event, in 1949.[9]

Relations must have been deteriorating between Sultān and Imām as the latter grew older, no doubt due to his increasing frailty, and consequent loosening of authority. The Saudis attempted to take over Bureimi in 1952 AD/ 1371 AH; as the agent of the Imām, Ṭālib bin ᶜAlī came to Muscat to discuss the incursion, but then went himself to Saudi Arabia, and the Imām sent an angry letter to the Sultān, denying any authority to Ṭālib. Twice the Imām asked for treatment in Nizwah from Dr Thoms, but the Doctor reported: 'the Muscat government forbade the trip, for political reasons.' But in the same Mission Report, the first of 1954, it was recorded:

> Now, however the government itself has issued the invitation, and we hope to go between Thanksgiving and Christmas ('53). The Imām is disturbed over his increasing blindness due to cataracts...[10]

According to Wendell Phillips, who was Economic Adviser and Representative of Sultān Saᶜīd, the Sultān issued the invitation, referring to the Imām as 'his old friend who was much honoured in all of Oman.' Dr Thoms went,

> wearing Arab clothes and observing Arab etiquette as the Imām had requested him to do. The operation was successful but the Imām did not live long to enjoy the restored sight of his right eye, for in 1954 he died.[11]

The visit is more fully described in a letter to me (22nd July 1990) by the wife of Dr Wells Thoms, Beth Thoms Dickson. She records the Doctor's final visit to minister to the Imām:

> My going to Nizwah with Wells was no guarantee I would meet the Imām, Arab attitude towards women being what it is.... I not only saw him, but he shook hands with me and spoke to me. I was pleasantly surprised by his open, friendly unostentatious manner... Sheikh Sulaiman knew Wells, he had been a patient of his and trusted him; he was also a son-in-law of the Imām The two of them administered justice in the interior, going together to villages to settle disputes over water rights etc. They had the reputation of making just decisions.
>
> The Imām had advanced cataracts. He no longer could read the Qur'ān. The native medicines and the Arabs who treated him were ineffective. Shaikh Suleiman urged him to call on Wells. So the Imām wrote to the Sultān asking him to request Wells to operate on him in Nizwah where he lived. This the Sultān did and Wells set about planning the tour.
>
> It was November 1952. Our 14 year old daughter Lois was home from Boarding School for the long winter vacation. She and I were included in the tour personnel along with hospital staff. The Imām, Wells knew, was a sick man, and would need building up before surgery. This would necessitate a long stay during which time, Wells decided, we would set up a clinic for the people. Besides staff we had to take all the supplies - no pharmacy or drug stores anywhere there.
>
> We arrived in Nizwah after a three day trek by camel. We'd no sooner got our walking legs than we were taken to meet the Imām. His majlis was an upper room of the great Fort. We found him seated, Arab

fashion, on a pallet on the floor. He apologised for not rising, saying illness had greatly weakened him. He shook hands with us and greeted us warmly. To Lois, whose Arabic name is ᶜaṭīyah meaning gift, he said: 'ᶜaṭīyah hal ᶜaṭiyah' as he picked out a pomegranate from a tray of fruit beside him and handed it to her.

We were all put to work in the clinic while the Imām was getting treatment. He'd suffered from repeated bouts of malaria and from dysentery. People came to our clinic in great numbers. Every patient got a card to be used on each visit. On it was written the name, a number, a diagnosis, and prescription. He then made a small payment and got his/ her medicine. On the back of each card was a Bible verse. We also had Bible tracts we gave to those who could read.

One day when Wells was with the Imām he said to Wells: 'You know the Mullah have complained to me about you, they don't like Bible verses to be on patients' cards and they are disturbed you are handing out Tracts. About the verses first. I asked the Mullah who came to complain -
"What does the verse say?"
He read "the fear of the Lord is the beginning of wisdom."
I said "What's wrong about that?"
He answered "It's from the Injil."
"Let it be" I told him, "it only points to the Qur'ān - you can tell the people that."
"Then about the tracts" he went on, "I suggest you sell them for a small sum instead of giving them away. Like any commodity in the Sūq if people buy, it's their choice." It was an amicable solution by a wise and tolerant leader.

The tracts went on sale for a few baiza coppers each. They were attractive and in good clear print. There was no reading matter around other than the Qur'ān. We were soon sold out. We found the booklets were being re-sold and for a higher price at each selling!

A small room with good light at the top of the Fort was set up for surgery. Gauze was hung in windows and doors for screening. A wooden door on struts was the operating table and a flashlight provided a strong beam where needed. The room was thoroughly sprayed with "Flit" as were all who were to enter. Not one fly of the millions around in that date-growing oasis survived in that room.

Surgery went without incident. The Imām recovered sight, and was able to read his Qur'ān again.'

The last sixteen years, of the rule of Sultān Saᶜīd was rarely peaceful. Ghālib bin ᶜAlī from the Hināwi tribe, was elected Imām, although the validity of the election was disputed by the Sultān. The real danger to the Sultanate lay in Ghālib's brother, Ṭālib, who had turned traitor in 1952. The Mission Reports were optimistic about the result 'In December 1955 the Sultān of Muscat and Oman won a bloodless victory over the Imāmate of Oman at Nizwah...' [12] In reality the oil company and tiny British forces between them had managed to 'influence' the garrisons of Ibri and Nizwah out of Ṭālib's control; at the end of 1954, a small force of Ṭālib's men surrendered to an even smaller force at Ibri.[13] The struggle continued for many years in the mountains, and was complicated by the emerging danger of Yemeni incursions from the south. Sultān Saᶜīd needed the support offered by the British, and the oil which, fortuitously, was struck 100 kilometres west of Nizwah. The spring 1957 Mission Report still spoke of the war continuing 'in a small area...' There was also a description of a visit to Tanuf for 'almost 100 trachoma operations...' and also of the state of the village just after their visit,[14] when it was bombed and strafed as a reprisal in the war; but the villagers had been previously warned, and were safe in numerous limestone caves nearby.[15]

The same Report had as its frontspiece, a photograph of 'the first (indigenous) Consistory of the Muscat Church'. Dr and Mrs Thoms had retired; with others, Dr and Mrs Bosch arrived in Oman, beginning an association that continues still. By 1962, the concern in several previous Mission Reports, was restated by American Pastors Kapenga and Dunham:

> The Mission looks forward to the day when there shall be a truly national Church of Christ in Oman. A church of Arab Christians supported by Arab Christians working with the world-wide Church.... We need responsible national leadership. What can we do as a Mission to help develop such leadership?... What do we leave that is permanent, lasting, should we have to leave tomorrow? The church MUST be indigenous... [16]

By 1970 AD/ 1390 AH, Sultān Saᶜīd had slowly gained ground, both militarily and politically, with mainly British military advisers, who were not afraid to get involved behind the scenes. Brigadier Colin Maxwell epitomises such men; Neil McLeod Innes, among several other chroniclers of these events, remembers him:

> At Ṣoḥār, I put up at the resthouse.... I sent a note across to the Commandant of the Bāṭinah Force, Capt. Colin Maxwell, he immediately invited me over to dinner. I found Colin then, as now, a delightful character. I have known no-one who has not liked him...

> He had arrived in Ṣoḥār the previous year to be greeted by the question from the Sultān: 'will you ride with me to Bureimi?' to which he had of course assented.... [17]
>
> Colin set out to explore the Ibri to Khabūrah route, avoiding the country of the Imām through Sumail with his headquarters at Nizwah. But going up the wrong wādī, Saudi occupation forces met him, and he was escorted to the Saudi commander. He was the best person to extricate himself from such a situation, no-one meeting him could doubt his integrity, he was the essence of goodwill. Common sense and a sound sense of humour displayed on both sides had won the day..... [18]

McLeod Innes describes Maxwell in action on the Rustāq road,[19] and a radio message to the Sultān, describing the 'fairly heavy fire' that he with his men was under.[20] Arriving near Nizwah, the Sultān greets Colin:

> all the way up my people have been greeting and congratulating me, but it is you, you and your men, who should be congratulated. It is you, and they, who have restored my country.[21]

Brigadier Maxwell was officially appointed Military Governor of the Jabal Akhḍar, or as Neil Innes put it 'Lord of the Green Mountain.[22]

Twenty-five years later, it was a high privilege for me to officiate at the funeral of Brigadier Maxwell. The high regard in which he was so obviously held, and the very deep love that he had for Oman when we prayed together before his death, made a deep impression on me. It was a great privilege, reading the twenty-third psalm, about the green pastures of God the Shepherd, at Colin's grave in the new Christian graveyard in a barren defile at Ra's al Hamrah; some of the many Omani officers, and hundreds of men were clearly moved together with myself.

But progress was not fast enough for the younger tamīmah and with British encouragement, Sultān Saᶜīd was eventually deposed in a bloodless coup, by his son Qaboos. The Sultanate of Oman, inaugurated in 1970 AD/ 1390 AH, is now 20 years old. National Day celebrations at the end of 1990 AD/ mid-1411 AH, were as flamboyant as for 10 and 15 years, despite the restraint still in operation after the boom years, and the looming war. But amazing material development has taken place, alongside a thorough educational programme, now producing many of the skills needed in a modern state. Up to 1970 AD/ 1390 AH, only a few of Oman's aspiring young men could find an outlet for their energies at home, and many had been working in other countries, such as Zanzibar. After the coup, the invitation to return home was clear, and many did.

Ṭālib, brother of Ghālib remains in exile in Saudi Arabia, having failed to raise the tribes of the Jabal Akhḍar. There is now no official talk of the Imāmate, although the present Grand Muftī, Sheikh Aḥmed al-Khalīlī, is related to Imām Moḥammad's predecessor. The present ʿulamā' have no apparent intentions of reviving the Imāmate. In 1989 AD/ 1409 AH, Sultān Qaboos led the prayers at the new Mosque at Nizwah, publically declaring his ultimate right to lead, or at least not to be led, in matters spiritual.

Considering that only two decades have passed, the Sultanate exercises a moderating influence through diplomacy. Behind the diplomats are Oman's businesslike armed forces; unlike most other Gulf States, Oman's military personnel are largely indigenous. To date, tension in Dhofar has continued, giving the Sultān of Oman's Land Forces (SOLF) and the Sultān of Oman's Air-force (SOAF) a real job to do in the south, and patrolling the Straits of Hormuz with SOAF and the Sultān of Oman's Navy (SON), during the Iran/ Iraq war kept the armed forces on their toes. Each year, more and more of Oman's towns and villages are connected by a metalled road system, the envy of many modern states. Gas from the oilfields de-salinates seawater sufficient to 'green' large areas of the Capital. As careful investment of oil revenues as anywhere, means developing agriculture and fisheries as well as some new industry.

Then there are all the Hospitals and Schools that have now been established in the most inaccessible areas of desert and mountain. Teachers are nearly always Muslim, Omani or Egyptian, but many hundreds of the hospital staff are Christians. This follows the decision made by the American Mission, when in 1971 AD/ 1391 AH they voluntarily turned over their medical institutions to the new government with the idea that missionaries would continue to work as part of government health programmes, rather than as staff members in private hospitals. That must have contributed to the fact that Christian services are allowed in all hospitals where requested, with of course the necessary care taken as guest-workers not to offend their hosts. I took another funeral in 1989 AD/ 1409 AH, which Omani government officials as well as many nationals attended; it was for Dr. Habel Das, who had begun as a mission doctor from India, and had transferred to government service in 1971 AD/ 1391 AH.

But the Consistory of the Muscat church has gone (see p. 71). As the Sultanate of Oman has opened itself to the rest of the Arabian world, so now for an Omani to be openly a Christian, is simply not acceptable. Freedom to worship exists for expatriates, in rooms in or near hospitals and work-camps all over the country, and on land given for church building by the present Sultān as well as his father.

What is now termed the Old Mission Church in Muscat, was built in its present form during the 1930's, and is dedicated to the memory of Peter Zwemer. The Muttrah Hospital opened a chapel in 1956 AD/ 1375 AH, which is still in use by ex-patriate congregations. The main Church site in Oman is at Ruwi, where a Roman Catholic Church and a Protestant/ Orthodox Church share a large compound with a number of priests' houses; this developed around a graveyard for British military personnel who died during the 1950-60's AD/ 1370-80's AH. A site was given by the Sultān for church building in Ṣalalah, the first ecumenical church for all Christian denominations. The most recent site to be given is at the eastern side of the Capital Area; the (Roman Catholic) Church of the Holy Spirit was consecrated in November 1988 AD/ 16 Rabia II 1409 AH, co-inciding with the 50th anniversary of the priesting of Father Maddi Barnabas, of the Capuchin - Franciscan Order. (He arrived at Bahrain in 1948 AD/ 1367 AH, and worked in Aden, Abu Dhabi - where he was involved in considerable building development - and Sharjah, before arriving in Muscat in 1974 AD/ 1394 AH, to oversee the completion of the Ruwi Roman Catholic Church). In November 1989, 19 Rabia II 1410, the Church of the Good Shepherd was consecrated, for use by Protestant and Orthodox Christians -see page 98.

The Christians who meet for worship come from many countries, the biggest group coming from India, and an increasing number of Philippino guest-workers swell the Christian congregations. Two Egyptian Arab priests quss, have small congregations, one Orthodox, one Protestant, for ex-patriate Christians. Denominationally, half of the 10,000 or so Easter communicants at the end of the 1980's would be Catholic, one-third would be Orthodox, one-sixth Protestant. Many of these communicants worship only once or twice a year, the public practice of their faith making little impact on their Omani hosts, other than perhaps confirming the belief that Islam is the only practical faith. For many Christians working away from the Capital Area, occasional church attendance is all that is possible, while some meet together in small groups, a freedom allowed in Oman. Sometimes, conscientious Christian workers are faced with the question from an Omani: 'What does your faith mean to you?' The final chapters attempt to identify pointers for relevant dialogue.

Notes and references:

1. NA/AC, 1941, 1st. Quarter, p.3
2. ibid. p. 5
3. PHILLIPS, Wendell, 1967, Oman, a History, Longmans, p.187

4. MAHLI, G. S., 1983, The Light of Oman, Green Prakashan, Jalandhar, 144002, India. Set at the time of Sultān Qaboos's accession, but making Dr Wells Thoms the resident doctor.
5. NA/AC, 1943, 3rd Quarter (vol. 201), pp.10-13
6. NA/AC, 1947, (only edition - vol. 211), p.4
7. NA/AC, 1944, 3rd Quarter (vol. 204), pp. 6-8; also 1951, 2nd Quarter (vol. 224), pp. 7-12
8. NA/AC, 1948, 3rd Quarter (vol. 214), pp. 8-9, where 24 communicant members of the Muscat church are recorded, 13 who had been Muslim.
9. NA/AC, 1949, 1st Quarter (vol. 216), pp. 13-15, including a photograph of Sultān Sa'īd cutting the ribbon. He clearly did not have the same fears as the Imām: Wendell Phillips in Oman, a History op. cit., p.188, reports a battle of wits between Dr Thoms, who wanted to take the photograph of the Imām, and the Imām who did not want his photograph taken. 'If I take the picture of you, the blame will be on me' said the Doctor. ' To this the Imām replied: ma'awanak bi-sharr, 'I will not help you in doing evil.
10. NA/AC, 1954, 1st Quarter (vol. 235), p.17
11. PHILLIPS, Wendell, Oman, a History, op. cit., p.188
12. NA/AC, 1955, Winter Quarter (vol. 242), p.14
13. HENDERSON, Edward, 1988, This strange eventful history, Quartet books, London, p.132
14. NA/AC, 1958, Autumn Quarter (vol. 246), p.15
15. PHILLIPS, Wendell, Oman, a History, op. cit., p.211
16. NA/AC, 1962, March (vol. 250), pp. 8-9. The last report in this 70 year collection.
17. McLEOD INNES, Neil, 1987, Minister in Oman, Oleander Press, p.37
18. ibid. p.99
19. ibid. p.144
20. ibid. p.156
21. ibid. p.162
22. ibid. p. 275

9: Dialogue: Folk Religion in Oman.

As this study has sketched the attempts during the last century of Christian Missionaries to establish an indigenous church in Oman, against 1400 years background of the practice of Ibāḍī tenets of Islām, both Christian and Muslim dedication to their respective causes is clearly revealed. There has been the steady development of mutual respect, which should augur well for future dialogue. This is unlike the experiences of Christian missionaries by some other Muslim communities; as Khurshid Aḥmad wrote in a recent editorial of the International Review of Mission:

> With the arrival of the Christian missionaries in the company of the European colonisers, a new chapter began in Muslim-Christian relationships. That some of them might have been motivated by the best of spiritual intentions is not among the points in dispute. But the overall Muslim experience of the Christian mission was such that it failed to commend itself as something noble and holy...[1]

No doubt Christians in Oman could lose the respect won at such cost by the American Missionaries. They could lose their own freedom to practise their faith privately, if they behave in an uneducated and rude way.

Omanis ask Christians what they believe, in modern Oman, as did Imām Muḥammad al-Khalīlī of Dr Wells Thoms in 1940 AD/ 1359 AH. Such conversations are matched by those who, from a Christian background, ask Omanis what they believe; some, as the daily newspapers report nearly every week, become Muslim. As Christians continue to be invited to speak about their faith, the following points might be considered.

A fundamental point that does not need expansion, but is well to state at the outset, is that only if Christians, regardless of denomination, recognise their unity of faith, will there be any validity to what they say. As anywhere else, Omanis are sensitive to the unity of the house of Islām, Dār al-Islām; Ibāḍī among them will want to emphasise the purity of their own beliefs, but not at the cost of the non-Muslim perception of the unity of Islām. Neither can it be any other way within the Christian Church. Samuel Zwemer was certainly persuaded of this essential prerequisite for any kind of statement as to what the Gospel is about, lived out by Christians. His perception was that: 'Muslims are fully aware that our lack of unity is a real lack of strength.'[2]

In order to understand where an Omani questioner is coming from, there will need to be an understanding of Islām, particularly of Ibāḍī Islām, more particularly (despite the preceding paragraph) in the face of the assurance that: wherever other

Muslims may differ from Ibāḍī thinking, they are, inevitably, wrong! But if the 'People of the Book' can work at a better understanding of where the Ibāḍī come from, this will make future dialogue more fruitful.

Before considering implications for dialogue with Ibāḍī Islam as practised in Oman, which will be the concern of the last three chapters of this thesis, the impact of folk religion in Oman should not be ignored. It is not of course only Omanis who are influenced by folk religion; some Muslims from whatever background, have taken into their pattern of thought ideas that have little to do with official doctrine -in the same way that the religious thinking of many Christians is affected:

> It is important for Christians to research, study and assess the composite facets of official Islām. One of the major trends in the Islāmic world today, brought about by certain pressure groups from within the official religion, is the application of a more puritanical interpretation of the formal tenets of the faith... It is, however, equally important for Christians to get to know the less advertised but just as pervasive world of popular Islām. That world is discovered in the ḥadith literature, in the folklore of local communities, and in myths of origin. It is visibly worked out in rites of passage and at times of crisis... Behind the facade of established ritual worship lie beliefs and practices which reveal a strong commitment to an alternative view of the world.[3]

Fear from evil spirits has nothing to do with specific Ibāḍī doctrine, yet such fears are still felt by some Omanis; this no doubt has as much to do with East African sources as Arabian. Among some Omanis who raised the matter with me, such fears were obviously very real. It would be easy to respond with a materialistic contempt of such thinking, but New Testament narratives provide material for dialogue; like the healing of the blind and dumb man whose condition was attributed to evil spirits - Matthew 12:22ff; the healing of the demon-possessed daughter of a woman of Tyre - Matthew 15:21ff; Jesus commissioning his disciples to 'drive out evil spirits' - Matt. 10:1. Care must of course be taken not to use fear of evil spirits as a trick of proselytism. For myself, when visited by someone expressing a fear of evil spirits, I would go no further than to pray with them for deliverance. I would use the name of Jesus; in that he is a Qurānic prophet, and one well attested as having the power from God to heal (Sūrahs 3:49, and 5:113), I believe this was not an abuse of the hospitality offered to me by my host government.

Oman missionaries spoke occasionally of superstition, but concentrated on the physical healing of their patients. There is no doubt that they often used these and other accounts of Jesus' healing miracles in their teaching, but assumed their patients/ listeners would draw the conclusion that the healing offered them, while explainable from science, was still God's healing. I could only find two references to superstitious belief in sixty years of quarterly reports, and those only in passing; it was as if the missionaries 'played down' such thinking rather than capitalise on it.

However, the fertile interest of Samuel Zwemer in many aspects of belief across the Islāmic world, led him to investigation in "The Familiar Spirit, or Qarina" an article published in the Muslim World in 1916. Zwemer refers to several Quranic references to qarin, to a possible origin to the belief as found in the 'Book of the Dead' of ancient Egypt, as well as Muslim understanding of Muḥammad's teaching, concerning his own qarin, or qarinah.. Jesus too, Zwemer reports, had a qarin:

> 'As Jesus was sinless, and because, in accordance with the well-known tradition, Satan was unable to touch Him at His birth, His Qarinah like that of Muhammad was a good one. "On the authority of Ka'ab the Holy Spirit, Gabriel, strengthened Jesus because He was His qarin and constant companion, and went with Him wherever he went until the day when He was taken up to heaven." (see page 365 Kasus el Anbīyah by Eth Tha'alābi). While in the case of Muḥammad and Jesus and perhaps also in the case of other prophets, the qarin or qarinah was or became a good spirit, the general teaching is that all human beings, non-Muslims as well as Muslims, have their familiar spirit, who is in every case jealous, malignant, and the cause of physical and moral ill, save in as far as his influence is warded off by magic or religion...'[4]

Kenneth Cragg, in The Dome and the Rock also describes belief in the concept of qarin.[5] Bill Musk, in The Unseen Face of Islām, also notes the belief.[6] It is some form of double of the human individual, always of the same sex, frequently being credited with being the cause of trouble, sudden temper, sickness, even sterility.

Then there are named or un-named autonomous spirits -jinn, or more often for men, their jinnīyah, where it is 'not uncommon to describe a man as being married to his jinnīyah.' A belief in metamorphosis - by a jinn into an animal form - is one reason care is taken, particularly with dogs and cats. Such creatures are treated with caution, and God's protection may be invoked, just in case metamorphosis by a jinn has taken place. The book of Genesis in the Old Testament, has of course the serpent, straight-forwardly called Satan in the Qur'ān.[7] Satyrs appear in Leviticus and a nighthag in Isaiah.[8] Such ideas are therefore held in common with 'People of the Book.' Some Muslims believe that the qarin too, can metamorphose.

Ibāḍī teachers today, like the American missionaries, play down belief in the superstitious. 'The real world' is their concern, there is a wary attitude to too much metaphysical speculation (see page 93). Popular belief however, cannot be ignored

ignored for long in serious dialogue. A possible consequence of thinking about the qarin is touched upon in the final chapter.

Deceased saints are, as in most of the Islāmic world, venerated in Oman. Near Ṣalalah is what is claimed to be the tomb of Job. The mosque is next door, but the many visitors are attracted to it, and is an important place for prayer. Pilgrims would also seek to receive something of the barakah of this beautifully kept shrine.

Barakah, literally 'blessing', is a concept common to most religions. The Patriarchs, of the book of Genesis in the Bible, laid much store by barakah, where it is often virtually a physical reality - for instance, Isaac giving Jacob his blessing rather than Esau, or Jacob's blessing of his grandsons Ephraim and Manasseh.[9] Once given, a blessing cannot be taken away, the word is the same in Arabic and Hebrew. The text of the Qur'ān is considered particularly efficacious for building up barakah, and many amulets, whether on paper and sown into clothing, or engraved onto silver and worn as an ornament, are to be found in Oman. The ḥajj - pilgrimage - to Makkah is also an opportunity to receive blessing, where a physical embracing of the ka^{c}bah, and the drawing of Zamzam water is believed to transfer barakah. Kenneth Cragg says of it: 'Barakah cannot be had without touch....'

> It cannot be had without a personal relationship between the desire and the supply, between the need and the satisfaction. It becomes a very right and feasible parable of the nature of faith. Was it not just this aspect of superstition which motivated our Lord in his welcome to the mothers, and the woman with the issue of blood? He saw in their simple-minded reliance on touch a token of the wistfulness of true faith. All that has to do with barakah has within it this rich lesson, "Come unto me." Salvation is never a second-hand affair; it must be had by the person personally. Given the Christian truth of the ever-accessible universal lover, the superstitious impulse to access has its true answer. The cross is the cost and the assurance of the blessed accessibility of the blesser of all. It is the form in the heart of God of his open invitation to mankind.[10]

Whenever I raised in conversation, the question of the place of animal sacrifice within Ibāḍī thought, it has been dismissed as an irrelevant 'outside' influence; but for many Omanis, the place of sacrifice is important, and an observant traveller can hardly ignore such places, marked with coloured cloths on poles and rocks. James Cantine (page 63) records the sacrifices offered at the foundation-laying stage of the building of the permanent American Mission house in 1901-2 AD/ 1319-20 AH; such sacrifices continue throughout Oman, and at times of deliverance from danger, child-birth (the ᶜAqīqah sacrifice), the laying-down of a keel at a ship's launching, and at times of celebration such as marriage. Special sites for sacrifice are respected by local communities; with influences both from East Africa, and growing no doubt from greater contact with Islam in the rest of Arabia and the Middle East; but as far as I could ascertain, in the heartland of Ibāḍism, the Jabal Akhḍar, there were no such places. More work could well be done in exploring with the Ibāḍī, their own intellectual antipathy to such practice, alongside an attempt to say what is the Christian doctrine of Atonement. Such an approach towards Islām generally, was certainly advocated by Samuel Zwemer, with several articles, such as "The ᶜAqīqa Sacrifice", and "Atonement by Blood Sacrifice in Islām", in the Muslim World quarterly, in 1916 and 1946 respectively.[11] David Brown, before he became Anglican Bishop of Guildford (he died shortly after the failure of the Anglican/ Methodist Reunion Covenant in 1981) emphasised the link between the cross of Jesus and this 'redemption' sacrifice (see page 95). Following consideration of four doctrines of Ibāḍism, I will return to this theme when considering implications for dialogue. To conclude this chapter:

> One final thought. Is not superstition everywhere a sort of doubt about whether life in general cares about life in particular, whether "what is" really has room for "I am"? It is an underlying fear of life's emnity to me. So then its one sure antidote is that love of our neighbour, the seeking of his good in all circumstances, which we learn in what is superstition's final solvent, namely, the assurance of the love of God. Therein every Christian's compassion is in turn a means to the redemption of his fellow's fears. When our environment is known as the area of pure "philanthropy", this love of man for man banishes the bogeys of malevolence and blunts the ravages in unpredictable powers in nature and event.[12]

Kenneth Cragg could hardly have written specifically a more appropriate description for one hundred years of selfless service offered to the Omani community by the American Mission.

Notes and references:

1. KHURSHID, Ahmad, 1976, in the editorial of the International Review of Mission, Volume LXV, No. 260, p.367
2. ZWEMER, Samuel M., 1916, The disintegration of Islām, Fleming H.Revell Co., London and New York, p. 209
3. MUSK, Bill, 1979, The Unseen Face of Islām, Monarch, Eastbourne U.K., pp. 203/4
4. ZWEMER, Samuel M., 'The Familiar Spirit or Qarina', in MW, Vol. VI No.4, (Oct 1916) p. 365
5. CRAGG, Kenneth, 1964, The Dome on the Rock, SPCK London, p. 179

6. MUSK, Bill, The Unseen Face of Islām, op. cit., p. 180, p. 227, etc
7. Sūrah 20: 115-8
8. Leviticus 17:7, Isaiah 34:14
9. Genesis Chapter 48
10. CRAGG, Kenneth, The Dome and the Rock, op. cit., p. 181
11. ZWEMER, Samuel M., 'The ᶜAkīka Sacrifice', in MW, Vol. VI No.3, (July 1916), p.236, and 'Atonement by Blood sacrifice in Islām', in MW Vol. XXXVI (1946), pp. 189f
12. CRAGG, Kenneth, The Dome and the Rock, op. cit., p. 182

10: Distinctive Doctrines of Ibāḍism.

For the purpose of this chapter, I propose to focus on particular Ibāḍī doctrines, which not only distinguish adherents from other Muslims, but which I hope to show in the next chapter, have relevance for contemporary dialogue. The Revd G. P. Badger, highlights such doctrines, in his extensively edited translation of Salīl bin Razik's History of the Imāms and Seyyids of Oman, published in 1871. He provides an appendix 'On the Title of Imām,' where he sums up:

> The doctrines of the Ibādhiyah, as far as they are to be gathered from the Arabian authorities adduced in the foregoing dissertation, differ from those of the orthodox Muslims in three cardinal points. 1st. On the Imāmate... 2ndly. Predestination and Free Will... 3rdly. On the merit and demerit of human actions.... [1]

I shall follow Badger's century-old analysis, with a consideration of two doctrines highlighted by a modern scholar from Oman, Sheikh Aḥmed Hamoud Al-Maamiry; the interpretation of the Qur'ān, and the question of whether or not the face of God is ever to be seen. I shall consider possible implications of these doctrines, in the next chapter.

'...1st, on the Imāmate....' More recent commentators within and outside Ibāḍism would agree: the Ibāḍī share with the Kharijī the doctrine of Imām by election, which they claim was the original understanding of the Caliphate. The need for a leader to defend the true faith, to ensure as far as possible the reign of God on earth, and to unite the community of believers, is shared with other Muslims; like, for instance, the Sunni community, the Ibāḍī assert that any Muslim of good character, 'even an Abyssianian slave,' can become the Imām. Ibāḍī resist the pressure for dynastic succession, more strongly than most other Muslims. In addition, the Ibāḍī Imām, although he holds absolute power, can be deposed by a council of religious leaders - the Mashāyikh who elect him - if he strays from the straight and narrow. The Ibāḍī consider Abū Bakr and ᶜUmar legitimate a'imma, but that ᶜUthmān was only legitimate up to the seventh year of his reign. The rule of ᶜAlī is recognised up to the point of his agreement to arbitrate the battle of Ṣiffin. At this point he became apostate.

> The aim of the Ibāḍī is to restore the original unity of the umma through establishing true Imāmates which would eventually unite and reform the whole Muslim world.[2]

The various political circumstances in which the Ibāḍī found themselves in, caused them to develop four states of Imāmate existence: al-kitmān - or concealment, found during a time of persecution. In this state the election of the Imām is waived, and taqīyah - dissimulation on grounds of compulsion or threat of injury, literally fear or caution, may be practised. The Qur'ān Surah 3:28 (Al-i-'Imrān, the family of Imrān) is interpreted as giving sanction for this, but with the warning:

'....except by way
of precaution, that ye may
guard yourselves from them.
But God cautions you
(To remember) Himself;
For the final goal
Is to God.'

If during a period of al-kitmān the community existence is threatened, the mashāyikh may declare a second state of defence al-difāᶜ, during which a temporary Imām can be elected to carry out the task of combating the enemies of the community. During this time the third state of expansion shirah may be declared,[3] and in which special glory would be won by Ibāḍī who sacrificed their lives for the cause. The fourth state al-ẓuhur - manifestation, is reached when the political climate allows for the election and public declaration of an Imām. According to historic Ibāḍī doctrine, this state is achieved when the community has at least half as many men, arms, horses etc., as the enemy. The Imām elected in these circumstances is known as the Imām al-bayᶜa. He then becomes the supreme ruler who is obliged to govern the community on the basis of the Qur'ān and Sunna, following the example of Abu Bakr and ᶜUmar.

Theoretically, there could only be one Imām, but the geographical separation of the different communities sometimes led to several ruling at the same time, ie: there were several a'imma at one time, in Tāhart, in Oman and the Hadramawt. But for a time at least in the 8th Century AD/ 2nd Century AH, the Ibāḍī in the west and the east, accepted the universal Imāmate of the Rustamids.[4]

A chief ᶜālim at the end of the second century (A.H.) -Musa bin ᶜAlī described the ideal for the Imāmate:

> 'No army is raised, no banner held, no fighting men commanded, no legal punishments ḥuḍuḍ ordered, no judgement ḥukm given, except through the Imām. The Imām is an obligation farīda as shown by the consensus of the umma, muhajirun and ansar (i.e. the members of the original community.' The relationship between the Imām and his community is based on obedience to God's law as enunciated in the contract of election.[5]

Throughout the history of Ibāḍī Imāmates, there has been inevitable pressure to limit election to one tribe, or between two or three tribes who fight between themselves for the nomination. The Banu Rustām of Tāhart kept power within one family; but the Mashāyikh had the responsibility to depose if necessary, an Imām who ceased to be true to the Qur'ān, the Sunnah of the Prophet, and the example of the first Imām.

One of the reasons the Ibāḍī have been branded as Khawārij is their insistance that the Imām does not have to come from the Prophet's own tribe, the Quraish. This is the Sunni claim, and they see no reason why such a Qurashī cannot be acceptable to the Muslim community at large. This controversy resurfaced on an official level in a meeting in 1986 AD/ 1406 AH, between the Grand Muftī of Oman, Sheikh Aḥmed bin Ḥamed Al-Khalīlī, and the Saudi Minister of Justice, Sheikh Abdūl Azīz bin ᶜAbdullah bin Ba'az; challenged to a television debate, Sheikh Abdūl Aziz simply demanded that the Grand Muftī abandoned his own ideology, and adopted that of Sheikh Abdūl! [6] After all, Abū Bakr is on record as saying:

> 'O Community of Helpers - Ansar - in the name of God, we do not deny your generosity, and I have not preceded you in Islām, but the Arabs do not come together and do not listen nor obey except to a man from the Quraish....'

He is, however, later quoted by Abū Da'ud and Al-Tirmidhi, as recording the words of the Prophet:

> 'Whoever employs a person from a group wherein there is (another) one who is more agreeable to God has betrayed God, me and the Believers...'

So it is argued that:

> 'The Imāmate, therefore, cannot be determined on the basis of lineage and kinship, and the correct magnitude (standard of judging) is piety, knowledge, power and strength. When these qualities are available in the person of a Quraish, he will be more appropriate for the position; if not, then there should not be any consideration for the Quaraishī. The Prophet has said 'This is still with the Quaraishī as long as he does not provoke inventions and then God unveils him to them and reviles them as he reviles this improvisation.'

Sheikh Ahmed Ḥamoud Al-Maamiry, is the exponent of this view, in his revised Oman and Ibāḍism book.[7] It is of relevance, not only to historians, but to all those seeking understanding of, not only Arab unity, but an Islāmic community of Faith. A further possible consequence for the individual will be considered in the next Chapter.

After quoting views on the Imāmate as one distinguishing feature of Ibāḍī doctrine, G. P. Badger then lists as other features: Secondly, Predestination and

Free-will...' and: Thirdly, 'On the merit and demerit of human actions'. Perhaps his summary is arrived at rather too easily?

> 'Although the Sunnites differ greatly among themselves on these dogmas, the opinion more generally entertained among them is, that man has power and will to choose good and evil, and can moreover know that he shall be rewarded if he do well, and be punished if he do ill; but that depends, notwithstanding, on God's power, and willeth, if God will, but not otherwise. The Ibādhiyah, in the other hand, are charged with holding predestination in such a sense as to make God the author of evil as well as good...[8]

A contemporary commentator on the question would be Dr Muḥammad ᶜAbdūl Rauf. In 1970. he was writing from the Islamic Center of New York, on the issue of 'The Qur'ān and Free-will' in The Muslim World. Qadr - divine determinism, and the area of human deeds and human choices, is mapped out from the time of the burning of the Kaᶜba in 684 AD/ 64 AH, and the assault on Makkah by the Umayyads around 690 AD/ 70 AH. The question then was, 'had God willed these attacks -were they by the decree, the Qadr of God?' Rauf deduces the essential elements of the Qadarite position as: 'they admitted the validity of a doctrine of Qadr covering all divine creations, but excluding the area of human deeds.' He sees the Sunnī position as maintaining the term Qadr as 'a comprehensive concept, applicable both to divine and human deeds; excluding the area of human acts from the concept would be, in their view, a limitation inconsistent with God's omnipotence.' But as Dr. Rauf says:

> 'In our view, neither party was perfectly correct. The exclusion of human deeds from the concept of Qadr by the Qadarites was unnecessary for the protection of divine justice and the principle of human responsibility. It easily provoked their condemna-tion, and popularised the views of their opponents. Yet, the inconsistencies implicit in the harsh interpretation of the Sunnites, on the other hand, became apparent later when it was pushed to its conclusion... The term Qadr in its Qur'ānic use, is a comprehensive concept but does not infringe on human freedom.[9]

Perhaps such a summary represents Ibāḍī thinking rather more accurately than G. P. Badger. Several times in conversation, Ibāḍī friends revealed by their questioning as to what Christians believed on the matter, that they wished to reserve a large area for human freedom within their understanding of Qadr.

The Ibāḍī consider anyone who commits a major sin to be a Kāfir - unbeliever. This person is then expelled from the community. This is in contrast to other Khārijites, the Azariqah, who declared such a person to be a polytheist, Mushrik, which meant that his property was confiscated, his marriage annulled, (traditionally it was lawful to kill his wives and children) and he became a marked man, it was lawful to assassinate him isti^craḍ.[10] The Ibāḍī would not go so far, in the hope that the sinner might repent and thus be able to return to the community; a militant hostility is however maintained by the Ibāḍī towards the unrepentant. Again, a practical implication of this is considered in Chapter 10.

Sheikh Ahmed Ḥamoud Al-Maamiry would identify other differences that he believes to be of important in identifying the beliefs of the Ibāḍī. These would include: 'Interpreting the Qur'ān' and 'the Creation of the Qur'ān.' The Ibāḍī allow that the Qur'ān can be interpreted, by those 'firmly grounded in knowledge'. Such an approach is of course an important pre-supposition to serious dialogue. The Qur'ān, Sūrah 3:7 is given in support:

God it is who has sent down
To thee the Book;
In it are verses
Basic or fundamental
(of established meaning)
They are the foundation
of the Book; others
Are allegorical. But those
On whose hearts is perversity follow
The part thereof that is allegorical
Seeking discord, and searching
For its hidden meanings,
But no one knows
Its hidden meanings except God.
And those who are firmly grounded
In knowledge say: "We believe
In the Book; the whole of it
Is from our Lord:" and none
Will grasp the Message
Except men of understanding.

Yusuf ᶜAlī seems to go some way with the Ibāḍī position in his notes to the Qur'ān where he says:

> 'This passage gives an important clue to the interpretation of the Holy Qur'ān. Broadly speaking it may be divided into two portions, not given separately but intermingled; *viz.* (1) the nucleus or 'foundation of the Book', literally 'the mother of the Book', and (2) the part which is figurative, metaphorical, allegorical..... people of wisdom may get some light from it, noone should be dogmatic, as the final meaning is known to God alone'.[11]

So the Ibāḍī claim the authority to look behind apparent meanings of the text of the Qur'ān, to interpret it.

'The Creation of the Qur'ān': Sheikh Al-Maamiry recounts the story, that after the death of Jābir bin Zayd, a Jew called Abū Shakīr Al-Dissāny:

> 'ostensibly professed Islām with the intention of sowing seeds of discord among the Muslims, and declared that the Qur'ān was not created, but was eternal. After much debate, the ruling of the Ibāḍī scholars was that the teaching of Al-Dissany was false, and the Qur'ān was part of the created order.[12]

But it is admitted, the difference between the Ibāḍī and those for whom the Qur'ān is eternal, is 'only verbal', because such teaching simply emphasises that God is not dumb. It is with such a background, that an Ibāḍī Sheikh could come with an open mind, to the suggestion by a Christian, for example: that the Qur'ān in Surah 4:157 (Nisā' the Women) is not necessarily denying the death of Christ - see Chapter 11.

'Sighting God': - Is the Face of God ever to be seen? One issue which 'causes much controversy among Muslims is between those who say that God will be seen in the hereafter, and those, like the Ibāḍī, who say He will not.' But as Sheikh Al-Maamiry goes on to say:

> Discussing a subject like this is to dwell on the topic the knowledge of which (or the truth about which) does not benefit anyone, and similarly the ignorance of which does not harm anyone.[13]

He then defends the Ibāḍī position, quoting among many other Qur'ān passages, Sūrah 7:143 (A'rāf, the Heights). Here there is a narrative of Moses, not being able to see God. Mainstream scholars interpret this as being a limitation of sight only while in the mortal body, but the Ibāḍī maintain that this will continue in the hereafter. This aspect of Ibāḍī theology is further considered in the next chapter.

Al-Maamiry, in his recently revised work Oman and Ibāḍism lists several other doctrinal differences between the Ibāḍī and other Muslims, such as the Mediation (Intercession); the Balance (Justice); and Fear taqīyah (dissimulation), which links back to the debate on the Imāmate, and will be taken up in Chapter 11. It is prejudice however, that many Ibāḍī feel they are met with, when upholding their own tradition against the sheer numbers who support one of the larger groupings within Islām. The Grand Muftī of Oman, Sheikh Aḥmed bin Ḥamed Al-Khalīlī, replies to the question from an Ibāḍī student abroad about the status of his beliefs.

> Many people, because of futile publicity against Ibāḍism, warn against the circulation of their books; and this has resulted - with much regret - in ordering to burn these books in one of the Muslim countries.... Thank God anyway, that many people have now been inspired towards

this sect and are giving it reasonable consideration and are reading their books... I call on the Muslim youth to avoid fanaticism and sectarian tendencies which have ripped apart this community to such an extent that its enemies become discouraged to destroy it; and it has now become a follower instead of being a leader of the nations... I pray to God to grant us success.... [14]

Notes and References:

1. BADGER, op. cit., p. 394
2. WILKINSON, J. C., 1987, Imāmate Tradition of Oman, Cambridge University Press, p. 154
3. ibid., pp. 151, 155/6
4. EI², p. 658
5. WILKINSON, J. C., Imāmate Tradition of Oman, p154
6. KHALĪLĪ, Aḥmed bin Ḥamed Al-, Who are the Ibādhis? in a translation by Aḥmed Ḥamoud Al-Maamiry, published in Oman circa 1986, page 24
7. MAAMIRY, Aḥmed Ḥamoud Al-, Revised Edition 1989, Oman and Ibādhism, Lancers Books, New Delhi, p. 113
8. BADGER, op. cit., p.394
9. MW, Vol. LX July and October 1970, p. 296, article by RAUF, Muḥammad Abdūl, 'The Qur'ān and Free-will'
10. EI², p. 658
11. QUR'ĀN, footnote on p. 123
12. MAAMIRY, Aḥmed Ḥamoud Al-, Oman and Ibādhism, op cit. p.90
13. ibid. p.82
14. KHALĪLĪ, Aḥmed bin Ḥamed Al-, Who are the Ibādhis?, op. cit., last page

11: Dialogue with tenets of Ibāḍism.

In this chapter, I shall focus on the four doctrines identified in Chapter 10 - as having significance in Ibāḍī / Christian dialogue. A consideration of Apostasy, as it relates to thinking concerning the Imāmate; the place of Free-will in both Christian and Ibāḍī understanding; the reticence of Ibāḍī thinkers, to consider the possibility of one day seeing the Face of God; and a consideration of the Christian teaching about the crucifixion of Jesus as an example of Ibāḍī acceptance of at least the possiblity for interpretation of the Qur'ān.

The fact has to be faced, that a Muslim from any of the States of the Arabian Peninsula, can rarely these days be publicly known to be interested in, let alone convert, to Christianity, without very serious consequences. There is nothing new in that; the experience of Omani Christians was -after 1970 AD/ 1390 AH, the date that Sultan Qaboos deposed his father and inaugurated the Sultanate of Oman - that they knew growing pressure from contact with other Arabian States, simply not to be seen as Christians (see pp. 71 and 73). Such experience has been shared by Christian minorities since the dawn of Islām, even when their faith has been passed down for generations. When it is first generation, when an individual turns from Islām, then that is considered to be apostasy, for which the penalties are most serious.

The Ibāḍī position concerning apostates is not perhaps so final as for most Muslims, ie: allowing time for the apostate to return. It is relevant to state the more usual position: in The Law of Apostasy in Islām, Zwemer points to several Surahs in the Qur'ān which promise severe penalties without being specific; he quotes Sūrahs 4:90, 5:57, 16:108 and suggests also 2:217.[1] Several aḥadīth are quoted to support the death penalty for apostasy. Zwemer quotes from a paper issued by the Woking Mosque of 1922 AD / 1341 AH, which he follows with his own comment:

> 'We read of the putting to death of the party of ᶜUkl in our traditions, who, after professing Islām, feigned that the climate of Medinah was insalubrious, and being told to go to the place where the herds of camels belonging to the State were grazed, murdered the keepers and drove the herds along with them. They were charged under the crime of murder and dacoity, for which the punishment of death has been provided in Ch. 5:33 (Zwemer means Sūrah 5:35,36). This episode has generally been cited by the Qur'ānic commentators under the verse which ordains the death penalty for murder and dacoity; there is no other case which can ever be twisted to show that the punishment of death was ever inflicted in apostasy from Islām.'

> Zwemer retorts: 'We leave the reader to judge whether "this episode" given in every standard work on Tradition under the head of *"Apostates"* was recorded to illustrate the penalty for murder and robbery, or the penalty for apostasy'.[2]

Other and 'various books on jurisprudence used in Moslem law schools' are then quoted at length, as is Juynboll's Encyclopedia of Religion and Ethics which refers to other authorities.[3] The practice in Turkey is then quoted 'The law of Apostasy was naturally the law of the courts for many centuries...' and the way in which the British government in 1843-4 AD/ 1259-60 AH, obtained a pledge from the Sultān that death would no longer be the penalty for becoming a Christian (for someone previously a Muslim). Subsequent paragraphs argue that nothing changed however.

The cost of becoming a Christian from a Muslim background was one that Zwemer and others never under-rated, and referred to that cost in many articles in The Moslem World. In an editorial in October 1922, under the heading: 'Where the stones cry out' , Zwemer tells the story emotively, of the sentence of being buried alive in concrete that was carried out in Algiers, upon Geronimo in 1569 AD/ 977 AH. As an Arab baby Geronimo had been captured by Spanish raiders, and baptised; when eight years old he was recaptured by his relatives, and lived as a Muslim until, when he was 25, he returned again to the Christian settlement. Five years later he was involved in one more raid and was taken prisonner to Algiers and killed for refusing to renounce his Christian faith. The block in which he had been buried was broken 300 years later, his bones buried and a plaster-cast of his body now stands in the cathedral in Algiers.[4]

W.H.Temple Gairdner shared Zwemer's concern. He had arrived in Cairo in 1898 AD/ 1315 AH, and developed a life-work there as a Christian teacher with a deep concern for the Muslim world. He was incidentally a close friend of Samuel Zwemer; as an Anglican, Gairdner established with Zwemer a creative co-operation between the Reformed and Anglican Churches that continues today in the Gulf region, particularly in Oman with the Dual Chaplaincy there. Gairdner's pen was nearly as prolific as that of Zwemer. In one succinct article, 'Moḥammad without Camouflage', in The Moslem World, he recounts many examples of the severity with which Islām deals with those who do not yield to it.[5]

The Ibāḍī doctrine of the Imām and the conditions under which he may, or may not be elected, includes the possibility of al-kitmān, hiddenness, and taqīyah, dissimulation. These concepts clearly apply to the Community of Faith; it seems possible to also apply them to the individual, who, genuinely seeking 'The Way' to

God, and who decides the Christian Gospels to be that way. Presumably this would include belief, not only that Jesus died on the cross for sin (see subsequent discussion) but that the Christian doctrine of Incarnation is true, within a Trinitarian understanding of the Unity of God, (see final chapter). Could such an individual not have to declare their faith in public? Could an individual, with integrity before God, and in the light of the discussion to follow, maintain a personal taqīyah in relation to the community around them - within the meaning of Sūrah 3:28?

Let not the Believers
Take for friends or helpers
Unbelievers rather than
Believer: if any do that
In nothing will there be help
From God: except by way
Of precaution, that ye may
Guard yourselves from them.
But God cautions you
(To remember) Himself;
For the final goal
Is to God.

And, Sūrah 14:38 (Sūrah Ibrāhīm, or Abraham):

"O our Lord! truly Thou
Dost know what we conceal
And what we reveal:
For nothing whatever is hidden
From God, whether on earth
Or in heaven.

Such a solution to an old and often agonising dilemma, would not be new. Whatever airing it may have had, for generations prior to 1938 AD/ 1357 AH, the Missionary Conference at Tambaram (Madras) that year, certainly saw the possibility re-opened. Henry H. Riggs was openly advocating the views of William E. Hocking, professor of Philosophy at Harvard, and 'spokeman for the left wing of American Liberalism' who wanted a form of western Christian service to replace the traditional programme of Christian missions.[6] Riggs was Chairman of the Report of the Near East Christian Council Inquiry on the Evangelisation of Moslems in which it was agreed that

> 'followers of Jesus should be permitted to remain hidden disciples (rather than baptised converts) within the Muslim community. He advised against anything that 'the enquirer or his neighbour may interpret as clandestine efforts to alienate him from his own people...' One must strive to develop 'groups of followers of Jesus who are

> active in making him known to others, while remaining loyally a part of the social and political groups to which they belong in Islam' in hope that ultimately these secret believers may become an indigenous church group.[7]

As Lyle L. Vander Werff summarises in Christian Mission to Muslims - The Record:

> The ideas held by Riggs and expressed in the N.E.C.C. Report were openly rejected. A chorus of evangelical voices realised the dangers of confining mission to the permeation of Muslim society with Christian teachings and ideals; of postponing one's decision and the formation of the church as a visible witnessing community; and of accommodating the Gospel's call to repentance and discipleship.... The majority at Tambaram rejected the ideas set forth by Hocking and Riggs because the basic presupposition that "theological tenets are discovered by human experience" was not considered acceptable.[8]

The pages of The Moslem World in 1941 tell the story in more detail, as Riggs' article: 'Shall we try unbeaten paths in working for Moslems?' is matched by Zwemer's: 'The Dynamic of Evangelism.'[9] A fuller response was presented by Zwemer in The Cross above the Crescent; the validity, necessity and urgency of missions to Moslems.[10] Other books and articles continued to pour from his pen, until his death at the age of nearly 85, in 1952 AD/ 1371 AH. At Zwemer's internment, Dr Albertus Pieters said of him:

> ... in this case it is difficult to sorrow at all... he never yielded to the fashion of the day in toning down the atoning work of Christ or the peril of those who live without the Gospel...[11]

The dilemma remains however. Perhaps a short taqīyah would neither deny the Qur'ān in its essence, nor its conventional intepretation? It is likely that Zwemer would argue that a personal taqīyah is a position that a Muslim enquirer about Christianity could not maintain with integrity for long. Perhaps it could fulfill the teaching of Jesus, to ensure that before 'taking up the cross' the 'cost is counted.'[12] The other side of the argument from a New Testament perspective, which perhaps Zwemer would have pressed, is that much of the concern of the early church was, that Christians did not dissemble. He would surely have emphasised the words of Christ 'Let your yes be yes, your no be no.' In the chapter 'The Art of Being a Minority' in The Dome and the Rock, Kenneth Cragg compares the two Arabian explorers Richard Burton and Charles Doughty; the former disguised himself as an Afghani sheikh, the latter made no attempt at disguise. Cragg quotes favourably:

..."the instinct to imitate, to cloke your own convictions and follow alien and perhaps disliked conventions, is based on a deep distrust of human brotherhood." [13]

He goes on to commend the minority Christian community in a majority Muslim state, which does not attempt to hide.

Some Gulf States positively encourage dissimulation by expatriates, for instance when clergy or Christian missionaries travel under a job description such as 'teacher' or a business title; the real identity of the traveller is often known to the authorities; they simply turn a blind eye. The authorities of Ibāḍī Oman however, expect truthfulness.

One other practical aspect to the question of apostasy, is focused by the publication of the novel Satanic Verses by Salman Rushdie in 1988, and the call from around the Muslim world for the execution of the author on the grounds of apostasy. Previously it could have been assumed that modern mainstream Islām was playing down the ḥadith about the penalty for apostasy; such an assumption could perhaps be now judged as being premature. The Ibāḍī approach however, while condemning utterly either apostasy or anything that could be interpreted as an attack on Islām, would want to allow time for repentance. With the reported re-aspousal by Rushdie of his Muslim faith, such an approach could have been vindicated; but to date, the shīʿī authorities of Iran have kept the fatwah in force.

A discussion on Free-will (page 84ff), will nearly always surface in any dialogue between Muslim and Christian; and Omanis are no different. 'Is it written?' is an often-repeated question. There is work to be done by Christian theologians, in restating the Reformation doctrine of Predestination and Election, in the light of Muslim understanding, and particularly of Ibāḍī insights, where there seem to be parallels with extreme Calvinism.

An attempt to engage the Grand Muftī, Sheikh Aḥmed bin Ḥamed Al-Khalīlī, in such a debate, proved the necessity for much more informed groundwork. I put to him falteringly and through an interpreter, the premise that within the natural laws set by the Creator, human beings do enjoy free-will; and that difficulty arises only when we limit God's space and time as being no bigger in dimension than ours. I had in mind a speculation that I return to, in the final chapter, concerning Jesus and the Unity of God. The response of the Grand Muftī was to emphasise the need for reality, as against metaphysical speculation, in any future dialogue.

In The Dome and the Rock, Cragg's concern is about both the theological question of predestination and free-will; also with superstitious fatalism and emanciapation from such.

In the last analysis what matters is not bare exegesis, still less formal theology, but living relatedness, "alive-ness unto God". How do we help deliver the victims of a crude predestinarian fatalism? How do we confront men who are intoxicated with scientific "freedoms" with the truth that they are all the while accountable under law? How do we find the true identity of wills between ourselves and God, if "our wills are ours to make them his"? These are the questions that matter religiously when we have silenced, dismissed, or awakened the theologians.[14]

Cragg develops a parable on the theme of God as teacher -Al-Rabb - the Lord, and 'certain lines of recent Muslim thought' which argue that the term means the Nurturer, who educates and nourishes his children and leads them on through experience and error into maturity and stature:

...Human freedom, as understood in Christian faith, may be well compared to that which obtains in a well-ordered classroom, and such a comparison might invoke the notion of a divine "education" of man. The teacher in school is the unquestioned ultimate authority: it is he on whom the order and the purpose depend.... Within this president authority of the teacher, which never abdicates, there is a modicum of freedom for the children, an area in which they are permitted to be truly free agents even to the extent of being allowed to be in the wrong.... This is plainly the Qurānic situation. Islām itself, as submission, is not something capable of happening if God is all dominant. For in that event it is either unnecessary or impossible. There is a real sense in which to be genuinely muslim, man must be free....[15]

Concerning the third of the doctrines noted in Chapter 10, 'Interpreting the Qur'ān', Sheikh Maamiry suggests that those who are 'firmly grounded in knowledge' can begin the task (see page 86). It is with such a background, that an Ibāḍī Sheikh could come with an open mind, to the suggestion often made by Christians, that: the Qur'ān in Surah 4:157 (Nisa' the Women) is not necessarily denying the death of Christ:

That they said (in boast)
'We killed Christ Jesus
The Son of Mary,
The Apostle of God'
But they killed him not,
Nor crucified him,
But so it was made
To appear to them...

Could it be that this verse is simply emphasising the voluntary act by Jesus of laying down his own life? This would then simply be a commentary on the statement by Jesus recorded in the New Testament, John Chapter 10:18

> 'No man takes my life from me, but I lay it down of myself. I have power to lay it down, and I have power to take it again.'

Such an approach has been followed by Christian apologists to Muslims for many years; it is generated by a concern that challenges the heart of what Christians believe about Christ. It is well presented in The Cross of the Messiah by David Brown (1969). In his preface, he says:

> My Muslim friends have often explained to me the difficulties which they find in trying to understand the Christian explanation of the cross, and I have written therefore, with careful attention to their concern for God's sovereignty. It is my prayer that Muslims may be helped by this book to see in the story of the crucifixion, to which the Qur'ān bears witness, a "sign" of the eternal love of the God whose sovereignty they proclaim and serve.[16]

David Brown sums up the meaning of the crucifixion for Christians, but with an ear to Muslims. I quote in full the final paragraph of his chapter, 'The Theology of the Crucifixion' because he links my earlier highlighting of the ᶜaqīqah sacrifice, with the theme of my final chapter:

> Because all men sin, they all need deliverance, and this the Lord Jesus came to bring. He won his final triumph in his resurrection when he defeated death and rose triumphant over all the attacks which Satan and the forces of evil could make against him. His victory however, was not won for himself alone, and he gives it to those who follow, him, making it possible for them to serve God in a new way and freed from the power of evil. This truth is expressed in the word "redemption", which is taken from the practice, current at that time, of "redeeming" those who had lost their freedom, either through poverty or because they had been taken prisoners in battle: for the payment of a sum of money, or in exchange for other goods, the slave or prisoner could be "redeemed" or bought back", and, as a result, return to the status of a free man. In the Jewish Law the practice of redemption also had a religious significance: first-born children were "redeemed" from too costly a dedication to God's service by sacrifice (see Exodus 34: 19-20) Using the figure of speech, the Messiah said that he had come "to give his life to redeem many people" (Mark 10:45), that is to say, to set them free from the power of evil by his victory over Satan and over the powers of evil and of death. He won his victory by receiving in his own person the attacks of evil, and by bearing and

carrying them without failing or turning aside from the path of obedience to God; like a good shepherd whose sheep are attacked by wolves, he gave his life on behalf of others so that they might live (John 10:7-17).[17]

The Ibāḍī maintains with other Muslims, the standard interpretation of the Nisā' Surah, and believes that Christians had just got it wrong. Sheikh Maamiry for instance, favours the claim of the apocryphral Gospel of Barnabas, that someone else was crucified in the place of Jesus.[18] There is no doubt that among many Muslims today, the Gospel of Barnabas is judged as being close to the Qur'ān in its teaching about Jesus; it is therefore commonly held to be more authentic than the four Gospel accounts of the New Testament. An appendix is attached to the thesis on this subject.

Assuming dialogue can move to the point of an open attitude to the possible reliability of the New Testament Gospels, then the work undertaken by the Revd William T. Long, in his recent Durham University M.A. Thesis: Christian Responses to Islāmic Christology: A critique of Sūrahs Three, Four and Nineteen of the Qur'ān, would be a useful tool. His thesis argues that there is substantial agreement between the Qur'ān and the Bible with regard to Jesus, (ie the events of his death); while he does however, see limitations in dialogue based on textual comparison, with regard to the Christian doctrine of the Incarnation.[19]

If and when a Muslim in dialogue, could allow the Christian claim that Jesus died on the cross and rose again and that such a claim is not necessarily ruled out by the Qur'ān, then there is scope for Muslim and Christian to seek further for common understanding as to the unity of God, a theological understanding which is inevitably at the heart of mission - to make God known. The final chapter attempts a tentative 'sketch' for such a debate.

It is a debate that must be fed by an understanding of nuance of the Arabic of the Qur'ān. An exchange of correspondence with Kenneth Cragg illustrates this, arising out of a concern for a difference in translation between The Holy Qur'ān - Text, Translation and Commentary by Yusuf Alī, and Readings in the Qur'ān by Kenneth Cragg. Cragg translates Sūrah 3:55

> Then God said: 'Jesus, I am causing you to die, and I will exalt you to myself...'[20]

while Yusuf Alī has it:

> Behold, God said:
> "O Jesus! I will take thee
> And raise thee to Myself...[21]

Sūrah 5:121 is however translated by Cragg with the phrase

As long as I (Jesus) was among them, I bore witness to them, and when you took me to yourself...[22]

supporting, in this instance, Yusuf Alī's translation.

Earlier this year, Cragg wrote in reply to my query:

Re Sūrah 3:56 - the crucial word is a passive force/ active form participle intensive from the root which means "to pay a debt." *'I (God) am calling you to your account"* is a recognised form of words for "to cause to die" (eg English: "he has gone to meet his maker.") The active verb is regularly used for "to pass away," ie - "to die." Yusuf Alī's version moves further away from that sense by using *"I will take thee to myself"* which is much freer. But it conveys the same meaning, except that the Arabic form does not allow some kind of "taking" (eg rapture) which is not "dying." This is confirmed by the following clause relating to "exaltation" ie "rising" - which would have been included in any *"taking to Myself."* In Sūrah 5:120 the same verb is used in the active past tense (Jesus speaking) with the same meaning, but here there is no following clause about "rapture" to let *"taking to Yourself"* be ambiguous, though if the two passages are read together that might be the case. I suppose in varying the translation I was following the rubric of the 1611 AD King James people who wrote in their Preface about not necessarily rendering identical terms in an identical way (see Readings, p. 55).

On the whole vexed question of Jesus' "death"? I tried to write fully in Jesus and the Muslim where your two texts had to be joined with the crucial one in 4:158 with its associations with Docetism and "apparentness." In both of your queried verses either translation would be viable, provided that in 3:56 we leave room for the form of what follows about "exaltation" or "raising.

While being beyond the scope of this thesis, Jesus and the Muslim is clearly an important resource book in continuing this dialogue.[23]

Finally, from Chapter 10: The Face of God. as I noted, the Ibāḍī do not believe they will see God face to face, even in Paradise. There is a general traditional dislike of images of any kind in Arab culture, even photographs have taken some getting used to, as in some other cultures. In a recent letter from a retired missionary couple, Midge and Jay Kapenga, who used to teach in the Muscat school, they wrote:

We tend to think of the Ibāḍī as the Quakers of Islām. They have been, until recently, really different from the rest of Islām. Their mosques were plain and unadorned, often without minarets.... They were very strict about using such things as pictures. In the old days a group of them came to Muscat, and complained to the Sultān about the government school having pictures of animals (used to teach the alphabet). They said the Mission school had no such pictures (probably because we didn't have money for them). When they did get to meet missionaries, they seemed to want to discuss religion and were not threatened by the presence of the mission or by the things we did.

The etched main window design, of the new Church of the Good Shepherd in Muscat, intentionally takes account of Ibāḍī sensibilities. A haloed shepherd with stigmata, is depicted rescuing a sheep from a mountainside (the actual mountains being seen through the clear glass behind); only the back of the shepherd is seen, reaching down to the sheep. The whole Good Shepherd theme was chosen as an alternative to a cross on the structure of the church building, so as to avoid as far as possible any offence to Muslims; certainly Ibāḍī friends who have visited the church seem to have appreciated the point.

The choice of theme and name was encouraged by Dr Ken Bailey, during the Gulf Churches Conference in Cyprus in February 1989. By then, building work was about to begin, the design outlined by me, and refined by the Chair of the Protestant Church building committee, Peter Harwood. It was not easy for the Church Council, with so many denominational differences within the congregations (for instance both a baptistry and font were built together), as well as wanting to build appropriately not only for current expatriate needs but for a future when congregations will be smaller. Six weeks before I left, I was privileged to be present at the consecration of the Good Shepherd Church, by the Bishop of Cyprus and the Gulf, the Rt Revd John Brown (see pp. 74).

Maurice S. Seale, writing in Volume LIV of The Muslim World, under the title 'The Image of God', quoting from Isaiah 40:25 in the Old Testament, then Clement of Alexandria (who died in 220 AD):

> Deutero-Isaiah "saw" that no image we would make would do justice to the One to whom our whole planet and all things was but "as the small dust of the balance." To anthropomorthise was to make an image totally unworthy of God; thus 'bosom of the Father in John's Gospel 1:18 referred to the invisibility and ineffableness of God, and the best name for God is 'depth.' [24]

Bishop Kenneth Cragg is 'enormously compelled' by the attention given by both the Qur'ān and the Bible, to the Face of God:

> 'You do your alms desiring the Face of God.... You are referring your giving to the divine magnanimity, so that the one reproaches the other.

> Or, you are not giving your alms to be admired by your neighbour, but in the cognisance of God, who judges your motives.... The Christian understanding begins with the Aaronic blessing 'The Lord lift upon you the light of His countenance and give you Peace...' Is this not which we have in mind when St Paul says: 'We have the light of the knowledge of the glory of God...' in the face of Jesus Christ? What a face is to a person, the place of identification, Jesus is to God.[25]

Humanising aspects of the nature of God is, to some degree, essential. If Islam generally is cautious about 'sighting God', and Ibāḍism specifically is dubious, then 'hearing God' makes a good entry-point for dialogue. The Qur'ān is considered of course to be the very Word of God. Gabriel is believed to have dictated to Muḥammad every word of the Qur'ān. It could perhaps be agreed that if humankind is too far from God to hear Him speak, but is able to receive 'second-hand' His written Word, then at least in Heaven we will hear the Voice of God? If with the sense of hearing we know the presence of God, then why not with the sense of sight?

Notes and references:

1. ZWEMER, Samuel M., 'The Law of Apostasy' in MW, Vol. 14 (October 1924) p 373. he quotes Sūrahs 4:90 and 16:108 correctly, but must mean 5:57, not 5:59, and 2:217, not 2:214. The article forms part of Chapter two, in The Law of Apostasy, Marshall Bros, London, 1925
2. ibid. p379-380
3. ibid. p383, where the reference is to: JUYNBOLL, Encyclopedia of Religion and Ethics, Vol. I, p. 625, referring to other authorities, especially Matthews, Michcat, Vol. II p. 177f; C. Snouck Hurgronje, Indische Gids. 1884, Vol. I, p. 794; and El-Dimishqi-Targamet ul-Umma fī Ikhtilaf al-A'imat. (p. 138, Bulaq ed. 1300.)
4. ZWEMER, Samuel M., 'Where The Stones Cry Out' in MW, Vol. XII (October 1922) p. 331-3
5. GAIRDNER, W. H., 'Moḥammed without Camouflage' in MW, Vol. IX (January 1919) page 25-57
6. WERFF, Lyle L. Vander, 1977, Christian Mission to Muslims - The Record, William Carey Library, South Pasadena, California, p.257
7. ibid., page 263, and footnote: 'These ideas are found in the Report of the near Eastern Christian Council Inquiry on the Evangelisation of Moslems Beirut 1938); H. H. Riggs, "Shall We Try Unbeaten Paths in Working for Moslems?" MW XXXI (1941), pp. 116-26

8. WERFF, Lyle L. Vander, Christian Mission to Muslims - The Record, p.265
9. RIGGS, H. H., "Shall We Try Unbeaten Paths in Working for Moslems?" MW XXXI (1941), pp. 116-26; and Zwemer, S.M., "The Dynamic of Evangelism", MW XXXI (1941), pp. 109-115
10. ZWEMER, S.M., The Cross above the Crescent: the validity, necessity and urgency of missions to Moslems Grand Rapids, 1941, pp 215ff
11. WILSON, J. Christy, 1952, Apostle to Islām, Grand Rapids, p.247
12. Gospel of Luke 14: 24-33
13. CRAGG, Kenneth, 1964, The Dome and the Rock, S.P.C.K., London, p. 227
14. ibid. p.168
15. ibid., p.169/70
16. BROWN, David, 1969, The Cross of the Messiah, Sheldon Press, London, preface.
17. ibid., pp. 56-7
18. MAAMIRY, Aḥmed Hamoud Al-, 1989, Jesus Christ as known by Muslims, Lancers Books, New Delhi, p. 45-69
19. LONG, William Thomas, 1988, Christian Responses to Islāmic Christology: A critique of Sūrahs Three, Four and Nineteenof the Qur'an, unpublished Durham University M.A. Thesis, see abstract and particularly ch. 4 & 5
20. CRAGG, Kenneth, 1988, Readings in the Qur'ān, Collins, London, p. 164
21. Qur'ān, p. 137
22. CRAGG, Kenneth, Readings in the Qur'ān, op. cit., p. 168
23. CRAGG, Kenneth, 1985, Jesus and the Muslim: an Exploration, George Allen and Unwin, London
24. SEALE, Morris S., 'The Image of God', in MW, Vol. LIV (Jan. 1964) pp 1-2
25. CRAGG, Bishop Kenneth, in unpublished notes from a meeting with me in Oxford, February 1991.

12: The House of Islām and of War (Dār al-Islām, Dār al-Ḥarb: and the Unity of God.

The meeting of Muslim and Christian in Oman, leads to the central question of all Muslim/Christian dialogue, how do we speak together, of the Unity of God? How can Jesus be considered in any other way than orthodox Islām views him? How can Christians maintain he is any other than the last but one of God's prophets? It is not simply a question to be left to academics, nor one that is relevant only for political peace, whether in Oman between Omani and expatriate, or in the wider Middle East between Muslim, usually in the large majority and Christian, usually in a tiny minority. It is a question for political peace in Britain, where growing harmony between races, cultures and religions is threatened by the new fundamentalism of religions. Kenneth Cragg would argue emphatically that it is a big question:

> ....the misconception about terms: the Christian faith in God as Father, Son and Holy Spirit is not a violation of faith in God's Unity. It is a way of understanding that Unity - a way, the Christian would go on to say, of safeguarding that unity. Perhaps our largest duty with the Muslim mind lies just here. For the Muslim, faith in God as Father, Son, and Holy Spirit does violence to the Divine Unity. For the Christian it expresses and illuminates the Deity. The Muslim sees the doctrine of the Trinity as incompatible with belief in the Unity of God. The Christian finds these not merely compatible but interdependent. The issue, Christianly understood, is not Trinity and Unity, but Trinity and atheism. The Church's faith in God is defined in this way as the form in which such a faith is finally possible in this world of mystery and evil.[1]

The whole of Arabia is considered by Muslims as a Mosque. Hence the Wahhābī of Saudi Arabia insist there can be no place for Christian Churches, and when embarrassingly, ruins of churches that precede Islām emerge from the desert sands, they are simply covered up and ignored (see pages 44/5). All the more surprising, and a sure sign of Ibāḍī tolerance, the fact that Christians in Oman are given permission to build Churches. There is a relaxed confidence that enables the Ibāḍī to engage in dialogue in his island home (see Chapter 1) in a way that most Muslims in other parts of the world find harder. Oman is the heart of Dār-al-Islām, the House, or Land of Islām. It is harder for the Christian to understand where the Muslim is coming from outside Arabia, or Muslim state such as Pakistan, when the Muslim is on the defensive, where he or she believes himself or herself to be living in the Dār-al-Ḥarb, the House, or Land of War. It is better to meet in the House of Islām than in the House of War. There is a necessity, as Cragg goes on to underline in The Call of the Minaret to learn Arabic for serious dialogue - and not just the vocabulary, but the idiom.

Such a concept, of the world being divided between Dār-al-Islām and Dār-al-Ḥarb, is not Qur'ānic, but ḥadīth trace the idea back to the Medinah period of the Prophet Muḥammad's life.[2] It does not of course necessarily refer to active war - jihād, but sharpens understanding of the real divisions, that many Christians at least, all too easily, but quite mistakenly, try to gloss over.

At least some Ībāḍī Muslims keep an open mind as to the Christian claim to believe in the Unity of God; this is illustrated in the conversation between Imām Muḥammad al-Khalīlī and Dr Wells Thoms (pp. 66/7). The Imām's lack of surprise at Dr Thoms reply, was no doubt conditioned by the Qur'ān Sūrah 3:64

> Say: 'O People of the Book!
> Come to common terms as between us and you;
> That we worship none but God;
> That we associate no partners with Him;
> That we erect not from among ourselves,
> Lords and Patrons other than God.'

Yusuf ᶜAlī states the general Muslim exposition of this verse:

> In the abstract, the People of the Book would agree to all three propositions. In practice they fail.[3]

This is not the understanding of Christian theologians who have struggled to explain to Muslims, how they believe in the Unity of God. To illustrate from just two: Hans Küng, and Kenneth Cragg.

Hans Küng sees the 'central dogma of Christianity' (the Trinity, and along with it, the Incarnation) to be both the point of departure and at the same time, of dialogue between Christian and Muslim. He commends Hermann Stieglecker's 'fine report on the theological controversies between Christians and Muslims' in The Teachings of Islām (1380AH, 1960 AD), and believes:

> compared with Judaism, so much weaker numerically) in competition with Islām... is not only because of Islām's great military, political and organisational strength, but... a major cause of this shortfall seems to have been the *inadequate rationale of the "Central Christian dogma..."* Internal conflict was obviously a second theological element, together with the inadequate case for the Trinity, behind the Christian world's inability to withstand pressure from Islām.[4]

Küng then faces the question: 'What does it mean to say God has a Son?' He points out how much closer Jesus was to a present-day Palestinian Arab than to Byzantine or European images of Jesus. He says:

> This Jewish Jesus had no more notion than a Muslim in our time would of weakening faith in the one God (breaking the First Commandment). "Why do you call me good? No one is good but God alone" (Mark 10:18) was his reaction when addressed as "Good Teacher."[5]

Yet Küng believes that in Jesus, something "more than Moses" more than the prophets made its appearance. Jesus

> not only talked about forgiving sin, about challenging every hallowed tradition and rule, about tearing down all the boundaries separating clean and unclean, just and unjust - he did all these things. And he proclaimed them not for "one day" and the future, but - amid eschatological portents - for "today" and "now." No wonder he was accused of blaspheming God, condemned, and *executed* (on this last point, as we have seen, the Qur'ān's image of Jesus is particularly in need of correction).[6]

So, after Jesus' death, and on the basis on their Easter experiences, the believing community began to use the title "Son" or "Son of God" for him:

> There was an inner logic and solid reasoning in giving the name "Son" to someone who called God his "Father"...[7]

Küng traces Old Testament precedents for the title "Son of God", in Psalm 2:7, Psalm 89: 26-27, and 2 Samuel 7:12-16, where Israel's King is appointed *"Son of Yahweh"*, in defending the Christian appellation of Jesus as God's son through his resurrection and exaltation. he says that

> there is no trace of physical/ sexual (or even metaphysical) procreation akin to that of the Old Arabian "daughters of God."
>
> In one of the oldest pre-Pauline professions of faith, cited in the introduction to Romans, it says: "designated Son of God in power... by his resurrection from the dead" (Romans 1:4) Elsewhere, in an echo of a royal psalm, Jesus is "begotten" as God's Son: "He [God] said to me [to the King, to the Messiah, and now to Jesus]: 'You are my son, today I have begotten you,'" (Psalm 2:7, Acts 13:33). "Begotten" as king, "Begotten" as the Anointed One (Messiah, Christ), as deputy and Son. By "today", the Acts of the Apostles unequivocally means not Christmas, but Easter, not the feast of the Incarnation, but that of Jesus' resurrection and exaltation, about which the Qur'ān, too, speaks quite clearly.[8]

Küng goes on to describe what he considers to be the 'specifically Christian element' of what the faith of Jewish Christians was to develop into, as:

1) In the New Testament, believing in God the Father means believing in the one God, a belief that Judaism, Christianity, and Islām all share... "Father" should not be understood literally, as opposed to "mother," but symbolically (or analogously)... "Father" is a patriarchal symbol (with maternal features) for a primordial, ultimate reality that transcends humanity and sexuality. That means - and the Qur'ān has a great deal to say on this - power and at the same time compassion, care as well as protection, dependency and security. Understandably, however, the Qur'ān, while it has ninety-nine names for Allah, avoids the name "Father", which from Muḥammad's standpoint was hopelessly compromised by the tribal religions of Arabia, with their belief in the children of the Gods.

2) Believing in the Son of God means believing in the revelation of the One God in the man Jesus of Nazareth. In the New Testament, Jesus Christ is primarily viewed not as an eternal, intradivine hypostasis, but as a human historical person concretely related to God: the ambassador, Messiah, word of the eternal God in human form.

3) Believing in the Holy Spirit means believing in God's power and might at work among human beings in this world.[9]

Küng further explains his understanding of how 'from the biblical viewpoint, the Holy Spirit is God himself' and quotes St Paul in 2 Corinthians 3:17, where 'The Lord is the Spirit....'

> Therefore the encounter with God, with Jesus Christ, and with the Spirit ultimately come down to one and the same encounter, as Paul says in the salutation: "The grace of the Lord Jesus Christ and the love of God and the fellowship of the Holy Spirit be with you all." (2 Corinthians 13:14)[10]

There is no doubt that Hans Küng is engaging in a most serious way in an issue at the heart of Christian/ Muslim dialogue. For many Christians however, what he himself accepts, seems to be approaching, if not repeating, adoptionist theology - ie, that God adopted Jesus.[11] For Küng, this would be at the point of Jesus' death and resurrection; it was traditionally maintained that Jesus 'became' God's Son at his baptism, as supported by the voice from heaven: 'This is my Son, the Beloved, with whom I am well pleased' as recorded in three Gospels, Matthew (3:17), Mark (1:11), and Luke (3:22). Küng seems to follow St Paul, as in Romans 1:3:

> The Gospel concerning his Son, who was descended from David according to the flesh and was declared to be Son of God with power

according to the spirit of holiness by resurrection from the dead, Jesus Christ our Lord...

Emil Brunner speaks for many however, when he says that while literally it would not be impossible to regard the Romans 1:3 text as supporting adoptionism...

> it would not harmonise with the rest of the statements of the Apostle, both in his earlier and his later writings. Not only in the Epistle to the Philippians and to the Colossians, but even the First Epistle to the Corinthians contain statements about the eternal Son of God (1 Corinthians 8:6) which cannot be reconciled with any Adoptionist view of that kind.[12]

While such debate is beyond the scope of this thesis to follow much further, I shall attempt a tentative 'next step', perhaps appropriate in dialogue in Oman, after considering briefly Kenneth Cragg's position.

Cragg approaches the subject by saying, as we have seen, it is in the Unity of God debate, that for the Christian, 'the largest duty with the Muslim mind lies.' He insists that "debate" about God is unseemly, that it is 'un-Islāmic and un-Christian as long as it is querulous, assertive or doctrinaire...' He quotes the Old Testament book of Job, Chapter 38:2, 'Who is this that darkens counsel by words without knowledge?' But:

> Let none suppose that the issues are unreal or that they can be avoided. If we shirk or silence them in the realm of God they will meet us elsewhere wherever we turn. We must banish the suspicion that a conspiracy of silence would better serve to peace. But when we venture into word and colloquy we must remember that the theme is God.[13]

Cragg traces how the Hebrews made the same stand against idolatry as did Muḥammad in defending the unity of God; and how it was emphatically the God of the Hebrews that Jesus pointed his followers to. Yet, quoting St John's Gospel Chapter 14:1 'You believe in God, believe also in me...' the question is posed: 'Why is the fact of Christ inseparable from a final understanding of God?' Personal revelation leading to fellowship is Cragg's answer - fellowship that then reveals the fact of evil; the tragic reality of humankind's waywardness is:

> ...implicit in the possibility of fellowship. For Man would not be a creature capable of responding to the Divine goodness, coming to him in revelation, unless he were also a creature capable of becoming a rebel against that goodness. Love and obedience cannot be compelled and remain truly themselves... Christianity seeks to learn what God, the sovereign Good, does in response to this astrayness and disobedience in man. It finds the answer in Christ. It believes that all

faiths, not least Islam, should be alive to this reality of insubordination, of disobedience, of un-islām, in the life of men in history.[14]

So then the question: 'Can God remain sovereign apart from redemption? - is seen to have an answer (which is the heart of Cragg's book, and the quintessence of his theology) in the 'whole idea of Messiahship...':

> the ideal of which varied widely as long as it was in prospect. When Christ came, fulfilling and transforming it, it was seen to mean suffering and the crown of thorns. The significance of Christ as the anointed Redeemer, born, teaching, suffering, dying, is the most formative element in the Christian doctrine of God.
>
> The contemporary generation after the Resurrection understood the Godward significance of their experience of Christ. They discovered the truth of His claim: "He that has seen me has seen the Father" (John 14:9). That God was in Christ was the only adequate hypothesis on which they could express and transmit what their experience of Christ had meant to them. So they spoke of Him as "the Word made flesh," "Son of Man" and "Son of God," "the Captain of their salvation," "the Author and Finisher of their Faith." Theirs was not the language of polytheists. These men were not idolators. They were responding to a profound experience of God. They could find, as monotheists, no other ground on which to explain what Christ has been to them and had done for all mankind. God was not less God, no less One, by this belief; he was more so. For the sin and disobedience, which formerly frustrated His purpose and defied His law, and which, uncorrected and permanent, would have constituted a contrary force unsubdued to good, had been triumphantly overcome, in a way which no punitive judgement could do. It is out of this realm of deed that Jesus had said to Jewish monotheists: "You believe in God, believe also in me." Can we in our turn finally believe in God sovereign and supreme without believing in some enterprise like that of "God in Christ reconciling the world to Himself"?[15]

At my meeting with Sheikh Aḥmed bin Ḥāmed Al-Khalīlī, the Grand Muftī of Oman (see page 93), I had suggested that God's space and time are bigger in dimension, than ours. This was not only to make a point about human free-will; my concern also was to 'test' the ground for dialogue about Jesus and God. (I should add, the meeting was primarily between the Grand Mufti and my Bishop, John of Cyprus and the Gulf). Since first reading Christ and Time by Oscar Cullman, I have been gripped by the concept of God's times - *kairoi* - being decisive in this world's time, chronology. Cullman refers to four epistles by St Paul, also to St Peter which all point to:

> the redemptive plan (οἰκονομια) of the mystery which before times eternal was hidden in God" "is *now revealed* to his saints, to whom he willed to make it known." (Ephesians 3:9, Colossians 1:26, Romans 16:25, Titus 1:2ff, 1 Peter 1:20)
>
> When Paul speaks of the "mystery," he means thereby the stages of the redemptive history. This expression, which is connected with the "redemptive plan," indicates that a special relationship was needed in order to gain this insight into God's plan.[16]

In The Christology of the New Testament Cullman develops this theme of redemptive history - *Heilsgeschichte*:

> The Path leads first of all from the many in progressive reduction to the one, and from this one, who represents the centre (of time), back to the many. It leads from creation to humanity, from humanity to Israel, from Israel to the 'remnant', from the 'remnant' to the incarnate Christ; then it leads from the incarnate Christ to the apostles, from the apostles to the Church, from the Church to the world and to the new creation.[17]

He goes on to say:

> The New Testament neither is able nor intends to give information about how we are to conceive the being of God beyond the history of revelation, about whether it really is a being in the philosophical sense. It intends rather to report the great event of God's revelation in Christ.[18]

Cullman adds the footnote: 'Criticism of my description of the New Testament understanding of time in Christ and Time has almost without exception not understood this.'

My premise is, that perhaps particularly in Oman, where the understanding of the Qur'ān concerning the spirit world is particularly noted, it may be appropriate to emphasise that the realities and understanding that we have of this world, are not all that exist; that is, (while as Oman's Grand Muftī rightly warns - speculation can be idle) the fact remains that the world that God inhabits, is much 'bigger', outside our world. Jesus and the Gospel writers are consistent with the Old Testament in emphasising the dangers of the occult; their message is that God is greater than all such powers. Jesus specifically claimed to have authority over demons, a claim recognised by Muslims generally; but, at the heart of the Gospel is the concept of God's world, God's Kingdom 'breaking in' to our world. This understanding of time, is to be found also in the Qur'ān. At the end of Sūrah 23, the ungodly appeal to God for another chance (similar to Dives, in the story that Jesus told, about Lazarus).

So, could it be useful in dialogue, to suggest that the Qarinah of Jesus (see page 78), existing of course outside our space and time, is no less than the Spirit of God? Such a suggestion will inevitably seem to fall into the trap that Sūrah 5:17 of the Qur'an warns against:

...In blasphemy indeed
Are those that say
That God is Christ
The son of Mary...

The suggestion could only be made within real friendship, based on the desire by the Christian, not to correct the Qur'ān, but to join with the Muslim in seeking to arrive at a correct interpretation. Mutual obligation to undertake the search is a big enough step; it is perhaps at this point that friendship demands silence, in the absence of any clear way forward. It can of course be said, that Muslims generally are willing to give to Jesus, as does the Qur'ān, the title 'a spirit of God'; but to say 'the Spirit of God' is something very different, as Yusuf Alī argues in his footnote to Sūrah 4:171 -

> a spirit proceeding from God, but not God: the life and the mission of Jesus were more limited than in the case of some other apostles, though we must pay equal honour to him as a man of God. The doctrines of Trinity, equality with God, and Sonship, are repudiated as blasphemies.[19]

Yet, despite the potential pitfalls of such a theory for the relationship between the human Jesus and the One God of eternity, in the light of Cullman's concept of this earth's 'times' being 'within', (smaller than?) God's time, I believe it could help dialogue particularly in Oman.

One other suggestion that could open the door in dialogue between Christian and Muslim, in this crucial area of difference about who Jesus is, comes from Nigeria. Jeremy Hinds, until recently with the Church Missionary Society, suggests that the 'hands of God' can be considered as the second and third persons of the Trinity? Together with my speculation concerning the Qarinah of Jesus, and no doubt other intriguing ideas, these become possible subjects for dialogue, within a friendship based on respect for the Qur'ān and the Muslim, and also mutual trust.

Hans Küng sees fruitful ground for dialogue around the concept of 'Jesus as the Servant - ʿabd - of God,' tracing in the theme in the synoptic Gospels particularly. Kenneth Cragg emphasises the importance of friendship based on service in any meaningful dialogue:

> Our response to human need will demonstrate and commend the Divine Love, without intruding upon the soul's response to the Christ it bespeaks and from Whom it derives. Only so will a truly Christian balance be maintained between the missionary aspects of "faith and works" - the faith of the receiver, the works of the sent. Misconceptions may persist. But in proportion as we can conceive of school, hospital, or clinic in these terms, the force of these misconceptions will be broken. In service the Gospel is implicit; in preaching it is explicit.[20]

The warning was sounded at the beginning of Chapter Nine, that all too easily Christian mission falls short of its ideals. Service can become no more than a cloke for imperialistic or at the least, condescending attitudes. Certainly, Christians have to recognise they do not have a monopoloy as to what service means, 'Islām is not apathetic to its human problems and our service must be alongside,' says Cragg, and goes on to acknowledge 'the new nationalism which is developing both the principle of state responsibility and its active fulfilment.'[21] He traces not only medical service, but service through refugee prorammes, education and literacy. But it is in medical service that still the most lasting opportunities will be found?

> Funds and buildings, even skills, are not all. The transforming concept of ministry is indispensable to a true house of healing. Governments as such, East or West, cannot, with all the will in the world, create an ideal hospital. They may provide the resources and the machinery, as also may private foundations and assistance programmes. But the personal devotion on which the hospital's activity as a community of love must turn can only be assured in that consecration to human need which is born of the Divine compassion.
>
> Such good will is no easy growth, no chance product. It comes in contemplation of the Cross, in the imitation of Christ, in the power that springs from the divine grace...[22]

The Muslim will have little problem with 'the imitation of Christ'. May it be, that the quality of serving love of Christians will be such, even sacrificially so, that 'contemplation of the Cross' can be considered as a legitimate fulfilling of the Qur'ānic picture, of Christ as the servant?

Cragg specifically points out the contribution made in India by the Missionary training hospitals of Ludhiana and Vellore. Many of their graduates are now in the city hospitals and wādī clinics scattered all over Oman. Men leave their wives and families, more often it is the women who leave their husbands and families at home in India and the Philippines, and while their main motive is to support family back home, through their service to sick Omanis they can be the building blocks for the 'community of love' that Cragg speaks about. I was greatly privileged to have been given, as a key part of my job as Chaplain in Oman, the visiting and encouraging of some very Christlike people, in medical-related ministry as well.

Communication between Muslim and Christian, even dynamic interchange in relation to their da'wah and mission respectively, has - mainly in the last century - been worked at in the parts of the world that are yet in the Dār al-Ḥarb -the House of war, ie, anywhere that is not the Dār al-Islām -the House of Islām. In such a situation, Muslims are perhaps necessarily on the defensive; but Oman, and the Ibāḍī Muslims there, are integrally part of the Dār al-Islām. Through their hospitable welcome, and if offered the same respect that Jesus offered to all those who came to him with an open mind, there is here a unique location and people, for open and frank exchange, which could be of enormous help in the Dār-al-Allah.

People who know Oman better than I, should have the last word, summing up how in Oman there has been a century of genuine service in the name of Christ, resulting in deep trust and lasting friendship. Midge and Jay Kapenga, write their letter to me:

> Presenting the Gospel to Muslims is not easy. We are convinced, after a life if the Gulf, that it can only be presented in the context of a real personal relationship, a real friendship, that includes sharing and expressing one's deepest religious feelings, questions and doubts. It is hard to have that kind of relationship, but that's what's needed. There is no easy answer. Monologue gets us all nowhere.

Notes and References:

1. CRAGG, Kenneth, 1964, The Call of the Minaret, Oxford University Press, 1964, pp. 307
2. EI², Vol. 2, pp. 126-7
3. Qur'ān, p.139
4. KÜNG, Hans, 1987, ed. Christianity and World Religions, Collins, London, p115
5. ibid, p. 117
6. ibid, p. 117
7. ibid, p. 117
8. ibid. p. 118
9. ibid. pp. 120-1
10. ibid. p. 121
11. ibid. p. 118

12. BRUNNER, Emil, p. 343
13. CRAGG, Kenneth, The Call of the Minaret, op. cit., p. 308
14. ibid, p. 311
15. ibid. p. 307
16. CULLMAN, Oscar, 1950, Christ and Time, SCM, London, p. 7
17. CULLMAN, Oscar, 1959, The Christology of the New Testament, SCM, London, pp. 324-5
18. ibid. p. 327
19. Qurān, p. 234
20. CRAGG, Kenneth, The Call of the Minaret, op. cit., p. 213
21. ibid. p. 226
22. ibid. p. 231

APPENDIX: The Gospel of Barnabas.

There was an epistle of Barnabas circulating alongside much other early apocryphal material; similarities occur between the theology of the Epistle of Barnabas and the New Testament Book of Hebrews. But no mention is made in the early centuries after Christ, of a gospel of Barnabas, until the Gelasian Decree appeared, which is traditionally attributed to Pope Gelasius I, 492-496 AD. This work is mainly an account of the Acts of the Council of Nicea in AD 325, and professes to be founded on an old manuscript in the house of Gelasius's father.[1] It lists among apocryphal gospels and epistles, the Gospel of Barnabas.

Western scholars agree that the complete Gelasian Decree cannot be earlier than the end of the sixth century AD, but that would still give it time to be circulating around the time of Mohammad. The Council of Nicea was primarily a defence by the Church of East and West uniting together, against the Christian heresy of Gnosticism. An article by James Cannon III, of Durham, North Carolina, U.S.A., appeared in The Muslim World in 1942 AD/ 1361 AH:

> 'The Gelasian Decree contains a list of permitted and forbidden books, and lists as forbidden "The Gospel of Barnabas." It is safe to assume that the ground of the prohibition was the supposed Gnostic teaching of the book, since the Decree itself was an anti-Gnostic document, and the name of this particular book appears in the list with other better known Gnostic material.... There is no known reference to the Gospel of Barnabas from the Gelasian Decree to the opening of the eighteenth century.... Of this lost Gnostic gospel but a single unimportant sentence in Greek has come down to us. A tradition asserts that when the alleged body of Barnabas was exhumed it had a copy of the Gospel by Matthew clasped to its breast, and that this gospel contained a denunciation of St Paul. This could obviously be, not the canonical gospel, but an apocryphal work claiming Matthew's authority. Incidentally, the present text of the Gospel of Barnabas contains in its opening and closing paragraphs a dissent from St Paul. All Gnostic literature made Paul the object of attack.[2]

James Cannon explains how Canon Lonsdale Ragg, later Archdeacon of Gibraltar (Jabal al-Tariq) and his wife Laura published in 1907 AD/ 1325 AH The Gospel of Barnabas, edited and translated from the Italian MS. in the Imperial Library at Vienna,[3] (referred to for the remainder of this appendix, as the G.B.V.):

> Their work gives the Italian text and the English translation on parallel pages, and in a lengthy introduction, summarises practically everything that is known about the document.... The manuscript used by Ragg

has been in the Hofbibliothek at Vienna since 1738 (AD/ 1151 AH). It came to that library along with the literary possessions of Prince Eugene of Savoy. It was presented to the Prince in 1713 (AD/ 1125 AH) by John Frederick Cramer. Jean Toland had borrowed it from Cramer in 1709 (AD/ 1121 AH). This seems to be all that is known about this Italian version.... No one has ever seen an original Arabic MS., nor is there any reason to think that any such version ever existed...

The Moslem contention is, of course, that Christians have suppressed this, the true Gospel, and that their own previous inability to produce it was due to this iniquitous Christian conduct.[4]

Cannon tells of how 76 years later, in 1784 AD/ 1198 AH, a Spanish copy of the Gospel of Barnabas was referred to by Dr White, Bampton Lecturer for that year. In 1850 AD/ 1267 AH, George Sale published The Koran; in his own Preface he stated that the Spanish translation had had a preface; he then quotes George Sale:

> The discoverer of the original ms. was a Christian monk called Fra Marino, who tells us that having accidentally met with a writing of Irenaeus (among others), wherein he speaks against St Paul, alleging, for his authority, the Gospel of Barnabas, he became exceeding desirous of finding this gospel; and that God, of His mercy, having made him very intimate with Pope Sixtus V, one day as they were together in that Pope's library his Holiness fell asleep, and he, to employ himself, reaching down a book to read, the first he laid his hand on proved to be the very Gospel he wanted. Overjoyed at his discovery, he scrupled not to hide his prize in his sleeve; and on the Pope's awakening, took leave of him, carrying with him that celestial treasure, by reading of which he became a convert to Mohammedanism.[5]

Cannon continues to quote from the work of Lonsdale and Laura Ragg, in their translation of the G.B.V. (presumably on the assumption that the Spanish version was translated from the Italian). The first paragraph asserts 'the true doctrine of Jesus has been greatly contaminated, and that it is the purpose of the writer to give a truthful account of Jesus' life and teachings...' The paper on which the manuscript has been preserved, Ragg claims, had a watermark such as was used in Italy in the sixteenth century (AD/ Tenth Century AH); the hand-writing was as used in Italy in the same period. Then:

> A very puzzling reference in Barnabas is that to a "jubilee" as falling once every hundred years.[6] There is no jubilee known to the Qur'ān,

and the Jewish year of jubilee as described in the Old Testament came at fifty-year intervals.... The first jubilee in 1300 (AD/ 700 AH) was to be followed by another in 100 years, in fact it was so financially successful that there was another 50 years later. This is the only period during which even a renegade Christian could have understood the jubilee in the sense used by Barnabas. All the other internal evidence accumulated by Ragg points to a sixteenth century date.[7]

James Cannon lists further 'inconsistencies and incongruities', concluding: 'The supposition that Dante is a possible source for Barnabas remains unchallenged....' Dante was the author of The Divine Comedy, and Miguel Asin, a Spanish Catholic scholar, published a book in 1926 AD/ 1345 AH, in which he argues that the G.B.V. drew from Dante's imagery, which in turn, Dante drew from Ibn Arabi, the Spanish Muslim mystic who died 25 years before Dante was born.[8]

A year after the Raggs published their English translation of the G.B.V., in 1908 AD/ 1326 AH, the first known Arabic (see Cannon above) and Urdu translations of the G.B.V. appeared,[9] and so began the dispute between Muslims and Christians about the authenticity of the G.B.V. Temple Gairdner, with Selim ᶜAbd'ul Ahad, had already published in Cairo 'The Gospel of Barnabas an Essay and Enquiry'. But:

> the wide approval and acceptance of the Gospel of Barnabas, Vienna library text) in several - not all -Muslim circles, has made it a religious issue between Muslims and Christians.[10]

Professor Jan Slomp sees the argument moving onto a new plain, when in 1977 AD/ 1397 AH, Luigi Cirillo wrote a doctoral thesis at the Sorbonne, on the subject of the authenticity of the G.B.V., which was followed in the same year by publication in Paris of: Evangile de Barnabe -Recherches sur la composition et l'origine par Luigi Cirillo, Texte en traduction par Luigi Cirillo et Michel Fremaux, Preface d'Henry Corbin. This, Slomp describes as

> the first major publication by scholars who are not directly involved themselves in the argument between Muslims and Christians, about the G.B.V.[11]

Slomp introduces his own critique of Dr Cirillo's book, in Islamo Christiana, with the opinion:

> We do not go astray if we state that academic rather than religious zeal was the motivating drive behind his (Cirillo's) book)...[12]

while he also allows

> The present author's (himself) angle of approach is no secret for those already interested in this subject. This may expose my approach to the suspicion that I am more guided by my 'Christian prejudice' than by

> scientific considerations. The same is true of course, *mutatis mutandis*, of Muslim defenders of the importance of the GBV...[13]

This explains the dilemma, which challenges both Christian and Muslims. For Christians, how do we separate the desire to defend our own faith from an open and unprejudiced study of history? The challenge is also to Muslims: for whom, with the arrival of the G.B.V. text, there seems to be evidence supporting old traditions - ie that Jesus was substituted by Judas on the cross - but which are not Qur'anic; again, is the G.B.V. history, or fiction?

What follows in Jan Slomp's article is likely to be convincing to a Christian standing with Slomp, who describes himself as a:

> ...committed Christian deeply convinced of the importance of being earnest about the four Gospels which the Church has received as the authentic witness to Jesus Christ. I am also considering with respect and sincerity Muhammad's witness to God in the Holy Qur'ān, which my Muslim friends have accepted as the very Word of God. For almost fourteen centuries the dispute or dialogue between Muslims and Christians has been based on these two convictions about Bible and Holy Qur'ān respectively.[14]

In a footnote, Slomp lists some of the Muslim scholars who agree with his own opinion that this 'gospel' is a forgery:

> ᶜAbbās Maḥmūd al- ᶜAqqād, the author of a biography of Jesus as quoted by Kenneth Cragg in the News Bulletin of the Near East Christian Council (Easter 1961) with translation of what ᶜAbbās Maḥmūd al- ᶜAqqād actually said. Sulayman Shahid in the Muslim journal, Impact, published in London in the issue of Jan. 10, 1974. Prof. E. R. Hambye in the issue of May 1975 of Islam and the Modern Age, published in New Delhi India. Prof. Mohammad Yaḥyā al-Hāṣimī in Études Arabes No. 48 Arabic text and translation by M. Borrmans. I have also received personal letters from Muslim scholars expressing their serious doubts about the authenticity of the G.B.V. I do not feel free to divulge their names.[15]

Professor Slomp sets out to 'let the historical and literary arguments provide their own evidence...' He explains how the authors - Cirillo, Fremeux and Corbin, provide the second major study in French on the subject, and how they follow the publication by the Dominican, Father Jacques Jomier O.P., of his offprint published by the Dominican Institute of Oriental Studies periodical Mélanges, in Cairo 1961 AD/ 1381 AH, which introduced the Barnabas question to French readers. Jomier was in fact responding to the challenge of the Sheikh of Al-Azhar, Professor Abu

Zahra, who had written in his Muḥādara fi l-Naṣrāniyya (Lectures about Christianity):

> The most significant service to render to the religions and to humanity would be that the church takes the trouble to study and refute it (the G.B.V.) and to bring us the proofs on which this refutation is based. (Jomier)[16]

Jomier repeats Cannon's record of George Sale's description (with the Spanish translation) of the discovery of the G.B.V. Jomier draws out the parallel story of the discovery of the book, of an incident in the book, chapter 191, where a similar story or legend seems to be projected back into the time of Jesus; both stories with a moral particularly directed to higher clergy in medieval Rome?[17]

Jan Slomp concludes his Introduction with a 'Commentary on chapter 12' of the French text of the G.B.V., which is an account of Jesus' first sermon, delivered, according to the G.B.V., in the temple at Jerusalem, by invitation of the priests. Again, it is hard to avoid the conclusion that much of the text is in fact dependent on the Qur'ān, and Muslim tradition.[18]

The main body of Slomp's article, is a chapter by chapter survey of Dr. Cirillo's book. Cirillo's final chapter seeks to clarify the difference between the G.B.V. (about which there is only one pre-medieval reference, ie in the Gelasian Decrees) and the Epistle or Letter of Barnabas. Cirillo mentions the Codex Sinaiticis (4th Century AD) and Codex Hierosolymitanus (1056 AD/ 448 AH), as sources for the Epistle; Jan Slomp notes the omission of reference to the Codex Corbeiensis at St Petersburg, which predates Codex Hierosolymitanus by 100 years, and is a unique Latin text of the Epistle. Cirillo mentions a Book (Kitāb) of Barnabas in a Maronite Codex Kitāb al-Huḍā, which contains a list of apocryphal books, one of them Kitab Barnabas. Slomp comments:

> The Arabic translation of a Syriac original of the Kitāb al-Huḍā was made in 1059 (AD/ 451 AH). It seems to me most likely that this Book of Barnabas is not the Gospel but the Epistle attributed to him, because it contains "teaching of the twelve apostles" (Cf. the Didache). The proximity of dates and places of the preserved codices mentioned above point in that direction. Dr Cirillo assumes, but cannot prove of course, that the original "Gospel of Barnabas" contained Judaeo-Christian teaching and therefore got lost! [19]

The outcome of this debate is important, because it is being assumed by Muslims defending the authenticity of the G.B.V., that some at least of these early references, are in fact to a gospel. For instance, a book circulated to many public libraries in Britain during the last ten years, Jesus. a Prophet of Islām, by

Muhammad ᶜAta ur-Rahim,[20] where it is simply taken for granted that references to the Epistle are in fact to the Gospel.

'Critical Evaluation' of Dr. Cirillo's work by Jan Slomp, begins with the conclusion that Jomier was correct about the origin of the G.B.V. - that it contains an islamicised late medieval gospel forgery; but then Slomp seeks to establish the *"ideal milieu" of the G.B.V."* It is, I suggest, this part of his work that Christians most particularly need to learn from. In summary, his argument is: that the Franciscan friar, Fra Marino (see page 113 above) could well have been one of the many thousands of victims of the medieval inquisitors (who used various means of torture as well as death as a means of persuading victims to become Christian), with every reason to look for a means to fight back at a system that had treated so many, so cruelly. Before he had been made Pope, Sixtus V had been Inquisitor at Venice (known there as da Montalto), and was extremely active in the field of forbidden books and book sellers....

> Pope Sixtus V was obviously fascinated by books. He built the beautiful still existing Vatican library. This library displays a conspicuously large portrait of his holiness surrounded by clergy which I noticed in a visit in March 1977. I think that Franciscan Friar Fra Marino of the preface to the Spanish edition (of G.B.V.) tried to take revenge upon the former inquisitor in Venice by recounting the finding of the Gospel of Barnabas in the papal library.

A footnote is added after:

> Gregorio Leti (the biographer of Sixtus V) relates that as Inquisitor, da Montalto even took action against members of his own Franciscan order in Venice.... Cf. Miguel de Epalza, La Tuḥfa, autobiografia y polemica islāmica contra el christianismo de ᶜAbdullāh al-Tarjumān (fra Anselmo Turmeda). Roma: Accademia Nazionale dei Linei, 1971. The author of the Tuḥfa was a converted Franciscan who took revenge on christianity. The Tuḥfa may have been a "model" for the Gospel of Barnabas.[21]

So Jan Slomp suggests, Fra Marino being a Spaniard by birth (Inquisitors had of course been very active in Spain as well) and later a convert to Islam, was similarly, and no doubt very understandably, motivated in writing the G.B.V., either on his own or with help from other sympathisers. Whether he had himself suffered directly at the hand of inquisitors, or simply wanted to stand with those who had, is another question. Either way, cruel methods used by the Church in proselysation, stands either directly or indirectly, as background to the emergence of the G.B.V.

Dante's Divine Comedy gives more evidence of virulent anti-Muslim feeling at this period; while Dante makes only passing reference to Muḥammad (in canto 28), it is one where he:

places the Prophet in that circle of hell reserved for those stained by the sin he calls *seminator di scandalo e di scisma...* Already in Dante's classic portrait, we find the image of the Muslim linked with revolting violence, distorted doctrine, a dangerous economic idea, and the tantalising hint of illicit sensuality....[22]

Dante's invective is, to say the very least, horrific; belonging to the same centuries as the Crusades, where Dante's descriptions of the worst human beings can do to each other was all too often made fact. Professor Harvey Cox traces the underlying problem further back, to the establishment of Constantine's eastern empire, where:

> For the Arabians, living on what were then the outskirts of the Eastern Empire, it marked a rejection not only of the non-Semitic catagories in which the doctrine of Christ's divinity were elaborated in the church councils (the "being of one substance with the father") but also the political hierarchy the doctrine helped to sanctify, especially in the Byzantine environment. When the Pantocrator Christ began to sacralise an empire in which the Arabians were the underdogs, their refusal of the doctrine made perfect sense. Alexander the Great had created the cultural imperium for which Christianity eventually supplied the sacred ideology. The Islāmic revolt against this system was a revolt not against the Gospel as Muslims understood it but against what Christianity had come to be. Islām's implacable insistence on one God not only freed thousands of people from their fear of the evil jinn and united the feuding tribes of Arabia (and later a vast part of the known world) but also became a counter-ideology to the political function that Christian trinitarianism was beginning to serve. No "rival truth claim" debate between Christians and Muslims can begin until this history is recognised.[23]

The writing of the G.B.V. then, is simply the tip of the ice-berg. While Jan Slomp concludes his thesis by again challenging the historical basis of the G.B.V. (having posed the question: if Muslims generally do not regard Mirza Ghulam Aḥmad, the founder the Ahmadiyya movement, as correctly teaching about Jesus - Mirza Ghulam's followers believe Jesus was crucified but swooned, recovered in the tomb, and migrated to Srinagar, where his tomb can be visited - then, he asks, why do Muslims so gladly accept pseudo-Barnabas' gospel, which contrary to the Qur'an, attributes Messiahship to Muḥammad? His final question is:

> Must we really believe the philosophy of history behind the G.B.V., namely that the three Abrahamic religions had to wait for 1900 years for its "truth" to be revealed in order to establish an "harmonia Abrahamica"?[24]

So: while from the above perspective of non-Muslim scholarship it may be summarised, that while there was a Gospel of Barnabas, which could have been circulating by 500 AD (given that the Galasian Decree was from Pope Gelasius I himself); that the text now circulating widely around the Muslim world was edited, if not nearly entirely composed, in the Middle Ages; while in dialogue, it could be useful to point out that not only does the G.B.V. seek to correct the testimony of the Gospels of the New Testament, but adds considerably to the Qur'ān as well (and should therefore not be taken too seriously); perhaps it is in Jan Slomp's work in trying to understand the *"milieu"* for the G.B.V., that the most long-lasting lesson should emerge.

The emergence of the G.B.V. should encourage Christians to begin dialogue from a position of seeking forgiveness for past hurts - of which there have been so very many. It is for Christians to live out, not what are in fact totally anti-Christian sentiments of superiority and cruelty, but a genuine service to Muslims, against which our mutual histories could perhaps then be viewed more objectively. Such certainly - as my thesis has attempted to describe briefly and which begins to explore its implications - such is the example of many Christians who believed themselves to have been called by God, to a lifetime's service in Oman.

Notes and references:

1. STANLEY, Arthur Penryn, pre-1908, Lectures on the history of the Eastern Church, J.M.Dent & Co, London, between 1861-1908, republished by the Everyman Library before 1908. Third edition edited by Rhys, Ernest, p. 98
2. CANNON III, James, 1942, 'The Gospel of Barnabas', in MW, Vol. XXXII (April) p.168
3. ibid. footnote on p.170, which quotes: RAGG, Canon Lonsdale and Laura, 1907, The Gospel of Barnabas,edited and translated from the Italian MS. in the Imperial Library at Vienna, Clarendon Press, Oxford
4. CANNON III, 'The Gospel of Barnabas', in MW, op. cit. p171
5. ibid. p.172
6. ibid. p.173, footnote quoting: RAGG, Canon Lonsdale and Laura, The Gospel of Barnabas, p.191
7. ibid (CANNON), p.173
8. ibid. p.175 footnote, quoting: ASIN, Miguel, 1926, Islam and the Divine Comedy, translated and abridged by Harold Sunderland, London, John Murrey, 1926

9. SLOMP, Jan, 1978, 'The Gospel in Dispute' - a critical evaluation of the first French translation with the Italian text and introduction of the so-called Gospel of Barnabas, Islamo Christiana Vol. 4, Pontificio Instituto di studi arabi, Rome, p. 68
10-13. ibid., p. 69
14-15. ibid. p. 68
16. ibid. p. 72
17. ibid. p. 74
18. ibid. pp. 78-80
19. ibid. p. 105
20. RAHIM, Muḥammad ᶜAta ur-, 1980, Jesus a prophet of Islām, Educational Press, Karachi
21. SLOMP, Jan, 'The Gospel in dispute', op. cit., p. 107
22. COX, Harvey, 1988, Many Mansions, Collins, London, p. 22-3
23. ibid., p. 30-1
24. SLOMP, Jan, "The Gospel in dispute", op. cit. p. 111

APPENDIX 2:

The 'East' Window of the Church of the Good Shepherd, Ghala, Muscat, (as seen from the outside - the design is in fact etched on to clear glass; from inside the real mountains are clearly viewed)

Below: Architect's impression of the Church of the Good Shepherd, Ghala, Muscat.

BIBLIOGRAPHY:

A. (i): PRIMARY SOURCES: BOOKS:

ᶜALĪ, A. Yusuf, 1975, Text Translation and Commentary of the Holy Qur'ān, Islamic Foundation, Leicester

BADGER, G.P., 1871, translated Salīl bin Razik History of the Imāms and Seyyids of Oman, see below under RAZIK

BROWN, David, 1969, The Cross of the Messiah, Sheldon Press, London

CANTINE, James, and ZWEMER, Samuel M., 1938, The Golden Milestone, Fleming H. Revell Co., London

CRAGG, A. Kenneth,

1956, The Call of the Minaret, Oxford University Press

1959, Sandals at the Mosque, SCM Press

1964, The Dome and the Rock, London, SPCK

1968, Christianity in World Perspective, Lutterworth

1985, Jesus and the Muslim: an Exploration, George Allen & Unwin, London

1988, Readings in the Qur'ān, selected and translated with an introductory essay, Collins, London

FARSI, Shāban Sāleḥ, 1980, Zanzibar, Historical Accounts, Islamic Publications, Lahore (written in 1955)

HAWLEY, D., 1989, Oman and its Renaissance, Stacey International, London (revised edition)

KHALĪLĪ, Aḥmed bin Ḥamed,

1989, The Spread of Ibādhism in Northern Africa, translated by A. H. Al-Maamiry, Oman

Undated, Who are the Ibādhis?, translated by A. H. Al-Maamiry, Oman

KENNEDY, Hugh, 1981, The early Abbāsid Caliphate, Croom Helm, London

KŰNG, Hans, 1987, ed. Christianity and World Religions, Collins, London

LONG, William Thomas, 1988, Christian Responses to Islāmic Christology; A critique of Sūrahs Three, Four and Nineteen of the Qur'ān, unpublished Durham University M.A. Thesis

MAAMIRY, Aḥmed Hamoud Al-,

1989, Oman and Ibādhism, Lancers Books,New Delhi, (revised edition)

1989, Jesus Christ as known by Muslims, Lancers Books, New Delhi

MUSK, Bill, 1989, The Unseen Face of Islām, MARC/ Monarch publications, Eastbourne, U.K.

RAZIK, Salil bin, 1871, History of the the Imāms and Seyyids of Oman, translated and edited by G. P. Badger London (new impression Darf publishers, London 1986)

SIRHAN, Sirhan bin Sa^cīd bin, 1874, Annals of Oman, Book VI, translated by Ross, E. C., Calcutta (new impression Oleander Press Cambridge, 1984

STEWART, Revd John, 1928, Nestorian Missionary Enterprise, the Story of a Church on Fire, Christian Literature Society for India, Madras, republished by Mar Marsai Press, Trichur, Kerala, 1961

^cUBAYDLĪ, Aḥmad, 1989, Early Islāmic Oman and Early Ibāḍism in the Arabic Sources, Cambridge Ph. D. Thesis

WERFF, Lyle L.Vander, 1977, Christian Mission to Muslims: the Record William Carey Library, 533 Hermosa St., South Pasadena 91030, USA

WATT, W. Montgomery, 1983, Islām and Christianity Today, Routledge and Kegan Paul, London

WILKINSON, J. C., 1987, The Imāmate Tradition of Oman, Cambridge, University Press

ZWEMER, Rev. Samuel M.,

1900, Arabia, the cradle of Islām, Oliphant, Anderson and Ferrier, Edinburgh and London

1907, Islām, a challenge to Faith, Student Volunteer Movement for Foreign Missions, New York

1916, The disintegration of Islām, Fleming H.Revell Co., London and New York

1918, Across the world of Islām, Fleming H. Revell Co., New York

1920, A Moslem seeker after God: showing Islām at its best in the life and teaching of Al Ghazali, mystic and theologian of the 11th Century, Fleming H. Revell Co., New York

1923, The Law of Apostasy, Marshall Bros, London,

1923, The Call to Prayer, Marshall Bros, London

1952, The Cross above the Crescent; the validity, necessity and urgency of missions to Moslems, Grand Rapids

A. (ii): PRIMARY SOURCES: JOURNALS AND ARTICLES:

CANNON III, James, 1942, 'The Gospel of Barnabas', M.W. vol.32, p. 167-178

CRAGG, A. Kenneth,

1953, 'The Arab World and the Christian Deposit', in International Review of Mission, vol. xliii, pp. 151-161

1956, 'The Qur'ān and the Christian Reader', M.W., vol. xlvi.

1957, 'Ramadan Prayers', M.W., vol. xlvii, pp. 210-38

1981, 'Greater is God', M.W., vol. lxxi, pp. 27-46

ENCYCLOPAEDIA OF ISLĀM, 1913-34, 1st edition, (EI[1]), E. J. Brill, Leiden, 4 volumes:

al-Ṣufrīya, vol. 4 (part 1), p. 498-9

ENCYCLOPAEDIA OF ISLAM, 1960-91, 2nd Edition, (EI[2]), E.J.Brill, Leiden, 6 vols. to date.

Aṭfiyāsh, Muh. b. Yusuf b. ᶜIsa b. Salih, vol. 1, p. 736

Azāriḳa, vol. 1, pp. 810-11

Dār-al-Ḥarb, vol. 2, p. 126

Dār-al-Islām, vol. 2, p. 127

Daᶜwa, vol. 2, pp. 168-70

Ḥarb, vol. 3, p. 180

Khāridjites, vol. 4, pp. 1074-77

ENNAMI, A. K., 1970, 'A description of new Ibāḍī documents from North Africa' in the Journal of Semitic Studies, Vol. 15, No. I, pp. 63-88

GAIRDNER, W. H. T., 1919, 'Mohammed without camouflage. Ecce Homo Arabicus' M.W. vol 9

HAIG, Lt-Col. Sir Wolseley, 1981, Comparative Tables of Islamic and Christian Dates, Kitab Bhavan, New Delhi

HOPGOOD, D., 1972, Editor of The Arabian Peninsula, Society and Politics, London, George Allen and Unwin Ltd., -includes chapters:

a) BATHURST, R. D., 'Maritime trade and Imamate government: two principal themes in the history of Oman to 1728';

b) KELLY, J. B., 'A Prevalence of Furies: Tribes, Politics and Religion in Oman and Trucial Oman';

c) WILKINSON, J. C., 'Origins of the Omani State'.

KHURSHID, Aḥmad, 1976, editorial of the International Review of Mission, Volume LXV, No. 260, October, pp. 365-9

NEGLECTED ARABIA/ARABIA CALLING, 1892-1962, (NA/AC, Quarterly Journal of the Arabian Mission of the Reformed Church in America, republished by Archive Editions, London 1988, from original material in the Gardner A. Sage Library, New Brunswick, New Jersey, USA.

THE MOSLEM WORLD, 1911-1937, THE MUSLIM WORLD after 1937, (M.W.), A Quarterly Review of Current Events, Literature and thought among Mohammedans and the the Progress of Christian Missions in Moslem Lands. Vols. I-VI, published by Christian Literature Society for India, London. Vols. VII-XXVII by Missionary Review Pub. Co., New York. Vols. XXVII- present, by Hartford Seminary Foundation, Hartford, Conn. ZWEMER (see below) served as Editor 1911-1938, and as co-editor with E. E. CALVERLEY 1938-47. K. CRAGG Editor 1952-60

RAUF, Dr Muḥammad Abdul, 1970, 'The Qur'ān and Free-will', M.W. Vol. 60, two articles pp 205-16, 289-299

SEALE, Morris S., 1964, 'The Image of God', M.W. Vol. 54, pp.1 - 2

SLOMP, Jan, 1978, 'The Gospel in Dispute, in Pontificio Instituto di studi arabi - Islamo christiana, vol. 4, Rome, pp. 67-112

ZWEMER, Samuel M., 1911-47, Ed. M.W. Among the articles, editorials and book reviews consulted, principally:
'The heart of our message' Vol 6, (1916) pp. 225-227
'The ᶜAkika Sacrifice' Vol. 6, (1916) pp 236-252
'The Familiar Spirit or Qarina' Vol. 6, (1916), pp. 360 - 374
'On taking hold of God' Vol 9 (1919) pp 221- 223
'The Urgency of the Hour' Vol. 9 (1919) pp 331-335
'Where the stones cry out' Vol 12 (1922) pp. 331-3
'The Love that will not let go' Vol 14 (1924) pp 331-3
'The Finality of Jesus Christ' Vol 24 (1934) pp. 324-9
'The Dynamic of Evangelism' Vol 31 (1941) pp. 109-115

B. (i): SECONDARY SOURCES: BOOKS:

ALLFREE, P.S., 1967, Warlords in Oman, Robert Hale, London
ASIN, Miguel, 1926, Islām and the Divine Comedy, translate and abridged by Harold Sunderland, John Murray, London
BOSCH, Donald and Eloise, 1973, Sea-shells of Oman, Longmans, London and New York
1989, Sea-Shells of Southern Arabia, Motivate Publishing, United Arab Emirates
BROCKELMANN, 1948, History of the Islāmic Peoples, trans. Routledge and Kegan Paul, London
BROWN, David,
1968, The Christian Scriptures, Sheldon Press, London
1976, A New Threshold, British Council of Churches
BRUNNER, Emil, 1952, The Christian Doctrine of Creation and Redemption, trans. Lutterworth press, London
CAMPENHAUSEN, Hans von, 1963, The Fathers of the Greek Church, A. and C. Black, London
CARTER, J. R. L., 1982, Tribes in Oman, Peninsular Publications, London
COX, Harvey, 1988, Many Mansions, Collins, London
CRAGG, A.Kenneth
1970, Alive to God, an anthology of Christian and Muslim prayers, O.U.P.
1976, The Wisdom of the Sufis, Sheldon Press, London
1977, The Christian and Other Religion, Mowbrays, London
1980, Peter and Paul meeting in Jerusalem, Eyre and Spottiswoode Ltd.
1984, Muḥammad and the Christian, a question of response, Dartman, Longman and Todd, London

CULLMAN, Oscar,
1959, The Christology of the New Testament, trans, SCM
1950, Christ and Time, trans, SCM. London
HARRISON, Paul W., 1943, Doctor in Arabia, Robert Hale, London
HAIG, C. A., 1902, Memories of the Life of General F. T. Haig by his wife, Marshall Brothers, London
HENDERSON, Edward, 1988, This strange eventful History, Quartet books, London
HOSKINS, Alan J., 1988, A Contract Officer in the Oman, D. J.Costell, Tunbridge Wells
HUSSEIN, M. Kamel, 1959, City of Wrong: a Friday in Jerusalem, trans, Djambatan, Amsterdam
LANDEN, R.G., 1967, Oman since 1856 - disruptive modernisation in a traditional Arab society, Princeton University Press
LICTENSTÄDTER, Ilse, 1976, Introduction to Classical Arabic Literature, Schocken, New York
LØKKEGAARD, F., 1950, Islāmic taxation in the Classic Period, Copenhagen
LYALL, Charles James, 1930, Translations of Ancient Arab Poetry, Columbia University Press, New York
MAHLI, G. S., 1983, The Light of Oman, Green Prakashan, Jalandhar, 144002, India
McLEOD INNES, Neil, 1987, Minister in Oman, Oleander Press
NEWBIGIN, Lesslie, A Faith for this One World?, SCM, London
PETERSEN, J.E., 1978, Oman in the Twentieth Century, Croom Helm, London
PHILLIPS, Wendell, 1967, Oman, a History, Longmans, London, first published by the Librairie du Liban, Beirut
RAGG, Canon Lonsdale and Laura, 1907, The Gospel of Barnabas, edited and translated from the Italian MS. in the Imperial Library at Vienna, Clarendon Press, Oxford
RAḤIM, Muhammad ᶜAta ur-, 1980, Jesus a prophet of Islām, Educational Press, Karachi
RISSO, Patricia, 1986, Oman and Muscat, Croom Helm, London
SEVERIN, Tim, 1982, The Sinbad Voyage, Hutchinson and Co., London
SKEET, Ian, 1985, Oman before 1970, the end of an era, Faber and Faber, London, (First published as Muscat and Oman,the end of an era 1974
STACEY, Vivienne, 1982, Thomas Valpy French - First Bishop of Lahore, Church Missionary Society, London
STANLEY, Arthur Penryn, 1908, Lectures on the history of the Eastern Church, J.M.Dent & Co, London, republished by the Everyman Library. Third edition edited by Ernest Rhys.
SWEETMAN, J. Windrow, 1967, Islām and Christian Theology, Lutterworth Press, London

TRIMINGHAM, J. Spencer, 1979, Christianity among the Arabs in Pre-Islāmic Times, Longman London
ULLAH, Najib, 1963, Islāmic Literature, Washington Square Press, New York
WILKINSON, J. C., 1977 Water and Tribal Settlement in South-East Arabia - a study of the aflaj of Oman, Clarendon, Oxford
WILSON, J. Christy, 1952, Apostle to Islām - a biography of Samuel M. Zwemer Baker Book House, Grand Rapids, Michigan, USA
WINSER, Nigel, 1989, The Sea of Sands and Mists, Royal Geographical Society, Century, Hutchinson, London

B. (ii): SECONDARY SOURCES: JOURNALS AND ARTICLES:

DALE, Canon Godfrey, 1915, The Vital Forces of Islam and Christianity - World Missionary Conference Continuation Committee,, ed. Humphrey Milford, Oxford University Press, - sixth article, pp. 193-212
EICKLEMAN, D.F., 1980, 'Religious Knowledge in Inner Oman' in Journal of Oman Studies Part 1, Volume 6, published in Oman, pp. 163-73
Geographical Journal, London, Vol IX, and 1901
National Geographic,USA, January 1911, and January 1991
PIRENNE, Jacqueline, 1985, 'The Incense Port of Moscha (Khor Rori) Dhofar, in Journal of Oman Studies Vol 1, pp. 81-97
RIGGS, H.H., 1941, 'Shall We Try Unbeaten Paths in Working for Moslems?' MW Vol. xxxi, pp. 116-126
ROBERTSON, Edwin, 1976, 'Kenneth Cragg: a Christian Imam' in Breakthrough, Christian Journals Ltd., Belfast, pp. 44-55
SMITH, Percy, 1922, The Ibādhites M.W., vol. xii, pp. 276-88
Times Atlas of World History, 1986, Times Books, London, pp. 104-5, and pp. 134-5
WILKINSON, J.C., 1975, 'The Julanda of Oman', in Journal of Oman Studies, Vol. 1, pp. 97-109